ATTITUDES TOWARD
THE HANDICAPPED

Publication Number 829

AMERICAN LECTURE SERIES®

A *Monograph in*

AMERICAN LECTURES IN SPECIAL EDUCATION

Edited by

MORRIS VAL JONES, Ph.D.

Sacramento State College
Sacramento, California

ATTITUDES TOWARD THE HANDICAPPED

A Comparison Between Europe and the United States

By

LEOPOLD D. LIPPMAN

*Director of Services for the Mentally
and Physically Handicapped
City of New York
New York, New York*

With a Foreword by

I. Ignacy Goldberg, Ed.D.

*Professor of Education
Department of Special Education
Teachers College, Columbia University
New York, New York*

73893

CHARLES C THOMAS • PUBLISHER
Springfield • Illinois • U.S.A.

Published and Distributed Throughout the World by

CHARLES C THOMAS • PUBLISHER

BANNERSTONE HOUSE

301–327 East Lawrence Ave., Springfield, Illinois, U.S.A.

NATCHEZ PLANTATION HOUSE

735 North Atlantic Boulevard, Fort Lauderdale, Florida, U.S.A.

© 1972, by CHARLES C THOMAS • PUBLISHER

Standard Book Number: 398-02341-7

Library of Congress Catalog Card Number: 74-169885

With THOMAS BOOKS *careful attention is given to all details of manufacturing and design. It is the Publisher's desire to present books that are satisfactory as to their physical qualities and artistic possibilities and appropriate for their particular use.* THOMAS BOOKS *will be true to those laws of quality that assure a good name and good will.*

Printed in the United States of America

CC-11

To the memory of

HENRY J. LIPPMAN

FOREWORD

WHEN CRITICAL IDEAS take root in one culture and news about them is disseminated elsewhere, an intellectual "gold rush" sometimes occurs that has enormous momentum. This phenomenon was observable in the recent awakening of American educators and psychologists to the developmental cognitive concepts of Piaget and the English open classroom approach. George Bereday, in his *Comparative Method in Education*, pointed out that in the late 1950's all American high school dropouts seemed sloppy, tee-shirted, life-adjusted mediocrities in contrast to their British counterparts, who appeared solid, steady, academic performers.

Yet, as one works with colleagues from other lands who, for example, aspire to transplant American educational ideas to their respective countries, one realizes that the process is neither simple nor automatic. It is very tempting to get excited about innovating practices away from home and to play the role of the rooster who upon discovering an ostrich egg in the barnyard, called the hens together and said, "Now, I don't want to complain, but I want you to see what some of the others are doing." As a confirmation of this illustration, the field of mental retardation has its own case in point.

During the 1960's, Americans discovered that the Scandinavian countries were much further advanced than we were in the care, education and rehabilitation of the mentally retarded. Many travelers, professionals and non-professionals, verified the fact that the Scandinavians were, indeed, in the vanguard. With energy and soul searching, many "retardationists" sought to close the gap between American and Scandinavian services. The initial attempt was to plant the seeds of the Scandinavian model in various parts of the United States. Unfortunately, these seeds often were in the form of buildings and programs that replicated the European experience.

Despite all these efforts, the care, education and rehabilitation of the mentally retarded in this country did not rapidly undergo a major metamorphosis, because, although the trappings changed, the heart of the program did not. What was not transplanted from Scandinavia was the "concern for the dignity of the individual, more attractive physical surroundings . . . in short, a greater respect for the individual . . . ," so aptly emphasized by Leopold Lippman in this book. Using his unusual ability to inquire, he found that people of Denmark, Sweden and some of the other countries accept the view that "society has a responsibility for the blind, the crippled, the aged, children—in fact, for all those who cannot care for themselves." He reminds us throughout this book that "acceptance of social responsibility for all of society's weaker and more dependent members is a part of the prevalent philosophy in those countries."

Mr. Lippman's valuable account confirms my contention that all other changes are *pro forma* in our work with the handicapped unless the underlying attitudes are changed first. This, I am sure, poses a vast and exciting challenge to those of us who want to provide more effective services in the United States.

I. IGNACY GOLDBERG

INTRODUCTION

Services for the mentally retarded in Europe have been the subject of much study and praise. We in America had heard about the humane treatment, the progressive programs, the community acceptance, the respect for human dignity which characterized these services.

The President's Panel on Mental Retardation dispatched Missions to several countries of Europe in 1961-62, and they confirmed and enriched the reports received from earlier travelers.

At the same time, we wrung our hands over the urgency of changing public attitudes on mental retardation in the United States in order to facilitate the development of more adequate state and local services for the retarded.

Drawing on my somewhat unusual combination of experience—in public relations and in mental retardation—I wondered whether there might be a significant relationship between the nature and quality of programs for the mentally retarded on the one hand and the attitudes (of influential leaders and of the "general public") in the European countries on the other. It occurred to me that if I could find a correlation, it might point to ways of changing attitudes and thereby to improvement of the lot of the mentally retarded in the United States.

It was my hope that the information to be gathered in Europe might provide clues as to (1) what relationship the attitudes might have to the development of effective services for the mentally retarded and (2) how to modify attitudes in the United States in order to bring about improvement of programs in this country.

With these thoughts as a base, I requested financial assistance from the Rosemary F. Dybwad International

Award Committee of the National Association for Retarded Children. (I had already been invited to deliver a report on California's proposed plan for guardianship of the mentally retarded, at the First Congress of the International Association for the Scientific Study of Mental Deficiency, held at Montpellier, France, in September, 1967.) NARC approved the award, and I went to work.

The first step was to explore what had already been done. Although there was a fair amount of material in print about services for the mentally retarded in Europe, there was surprisingly little about *attitudes,* either in this country or abroad.

The countries I had chosen to visit were Ireland, England, Denmark, Sweden and Norway. In addition, I spent most of my three days at the International Congress in Montpellier talking with persons I would not otherwise have been able to reach, professional and citizen leaders in mental retardation from many other countries.

My "research method" was essentially journalistic, rather than social-scientific. That is, I talked with knowledgeable people, both public officials and private citizens, working from a basic outline but allowing the discussions to evolve as the dynamics of the individual situation suggested.

With the cooperation of the persons I talked with, I took notes on the highlights of what they told me. In addition, with a portable recorder, I taped many of the interviews.

Although I had not planned to study the mental retardation programs as such, some of my hosts and informants were so insistent that I felt obliged to visit an institution here, a day care program there, a hostel in yet another place. I did not come away with any profound observations as to the quality of the programs, but my visits did give me additional insights into the quality and import of social attitudes on the provision of services in the various countries I explored. I also took the opportunity of casual contacts with cabdrivers, hotel personnel and an occasional relative, to test the man-in-the-street awareness of mental retardation as a social problem.

My survey of the mass media was purposeful in a limited measure. I did have the opportunity for direct interviews with journalists in the three Scandinavian countries; I also had the benefit of comments from mental retardation specialists as to the attitudes of the media of communication and their impact on public opinion.

Since returning from my European study trip in 1967, I have observed more closely, and with a new perspective, the attitudes of Americans toward the mentally retarded. There have been such obvious expressions of public opinion as petitions to local governing bodies to prevent the opening of workshops or residential centers; there has also been the less direct but no less real evidence of inadequate public appropriations, wretched staff-resident ratios in state institutions, and complacent acceptance of discrimination and mistreatment which we have the power to change but choose to allow.

The shocking contrast—within a few weeks, in 1967—between a Californian's observations in Denmark and a Dane's observations in California (recounted elsewhere in this book) was simply a dramatic epitome of the state of attitudes in the United States. It was not just California (although the expressed reactions of governmental leaders there were particularly crude and insensitive); the situation was not much different in Pennsylvania in 1969 or in New Jersey in 1970.

Attitudes toward the mentally retarded, as the theme of this book states, are part of a larger attitudinal pattern. This was the essence of what I learned in Europe. (The H-Day project in Sweden was the most vivid example.) But although I "learned" the lesson in 1967, it has taken several years for me to understand it. I have only recently absorbed the reality of the indivisibility of social attitudes. The rejection and infantilization of the mentally retarded, the thoughtless erection of architectural barriers against the physically disabled, the resistance to the recovered mentally ill and former convicts, the denigration of mothers who must accept public assistance to feed their children, the contemptuous treatment of older men and women who may no longer be completely self-reliant in our complex society—all are part of the attitudinal "set" in the United States which is so different from the respect for human interdependency that I saw in Europe, especially in Scandinavia.

ACKNOWLEDGMENTS

For WHATEVER success my study may have achieved, I owe many acknowledgments:

To the National Association for Retarded Children and its Rosemary F. Dybwad International Award Committee, for providing the funds which made the trip possible.

To the State of California for allowing me the time to make the trip and to explore the subject.

To Gunnar Dybwad, J.D., and Rosemary F. Dybwad, Ph.D., for their illuminating, insightful, detailed and patient guidance in the development, planning and execution of the project.

To Mrs. D.R. ("Danny") Gullikson, for free access to the magnificent Gullikson Collection of publications on mental retardation and for her generosity with her own time and ideas. Her untimely death in July 1970 deprived the mentally retarded of an energetic and unselfish friend, but the library she built with her own hands, funds and love will have lasting value.

To Mrs. Helen F. Herrick, Earl Raab, Mrs. Edwina Serventi, Ralph O'Neill, Dean Neil D. Warren, Pastor William G. Jeffs, Gerald F. Walsh and other friends who gave their ideas and encouragement to enhance the success of the effort.

To Harvey Stevens and Prof. A.D.B. Clarke, among other leaders of the International Association for the Scientific Study of Mental Deficiency, for enabling me to participate in the Congress at Montpellier and to meet many informed and stimulating people.

And, individually, and with deep appreciation, to each of the many wonderful people in Europe, all of them newly discovered in 1967. They are listed in the Appendix.

A number of the ideas in this book have been expressed, in somewhat different form, in various periodicals. For their cooperation in publishing, and for their permission to use here, I express my appreciation to:

American Association on Mental Deficiency: "Sweden Remembers—and Provides for—the Handicapped," *Mental Retardation*, August 1969; and "Deviancy: A Different Look," *Mental Retardation*, June 1970.

Council for Exceptional Children: "England's Comprehensive Schools: Analogy for Special Education?" *Exceptional Children*, December 1969.

National Public Relations Council of Health and Welfare Services: "Effective Services Depend on Public Attitudes," *Channels Forum*, December 15, 1969.

The Seattle Times: "Care for the Mentally Retarded: Are Europeans Doing Better?" *Seattle Times Magazine*, December 21, 1969.

L.D.L.

CONTENTS

ATTITUDES TOWARD
THE HANDICAPPED

Part I

HOW IT IS IN EUROPE

Chapter One

EUROPEAN ATTITUDES ON MENTAL RETARDATION

WHAT IS WRONG with the mentally retarded in the United States? Why are they making so little progress? Why is there so much dissatisfaction and dispute over how to deal with them? Why, in many parts of the country, do retarded children enter school later and leave earlier? Why are so few retarded adults productively employed? Why, in spite of all we do, are there still waiting lists for admission to state institutions, and complaints by families, and a general feeling that we are spending too much and accomplishing too little?

What is wrong with the mentally retarded in the United States is the rest of us—the public officials, the civic leaders and the average citizens who, by what we do or fail to do, make the decisions that shape the lives of the mentally retarded.

For years I had heard that in certain countries of Europe services for the mentally retarded were quite different than in the United States. Travelers had reported that more retarded people live and function effectively in their own communities; that even the severely retarded are able to hold jobs; that residential facilities are well designed and attractively furnished and afford some privacy to the individual; that retarded persons who need care in a residential center may go there with some hope of returning to community living some day, rather than remaining in the institution the rest of their lives.[1]

---

[1] President's Panel on Mental Retardation: "Report of the Mission to Denmark and Sweden," 1962. There was also a report of the Mission to England and Wales, but it has not been published.

All this sounded quite different from what I knew to be typical in most states in our own country. I wondered why. The question was, How can these older countries, with traditions going back centuries, and with limited resources, essay more and accomplish more than the great, affluent states of the United States? The answer, from a distance of some five thousand miles, seemed to be: A difference in attitude makes the difference in programs of service.

Then, in September 1967, I had the opportunity to go and see for myself. Drawing on my dual background in public opinion and mental retardation, and with the aid of a grant from the Rosemary F. Dybwad International Award Committee of the National Association for Retarded Children, I undertook to study the attitudes on mental retardation in several countries of Europe, in the hope of discovering the essential features which resulted in the better programs, and with the expectation that it might be possible to modify attitudes in the United States to the same end.[2] The hypothe-

---

[2] A few surveys have been conducted of attitudes on mental retardation, and more on mental health, here and in other countries. Among the published reports and analyses, the following are worth reviewing: Gottwald, Henry: *Public Awareness About Mental Retardation: A Survey and Analysis,* Eastern Michigan University, 1967; Minnesota Association for Retarded Children and the Minnesota Department of Public Welfare: *Mental Retardation in Minnesota: A Survey of Public Information and Attitudes,* 1962; Tri-State Comprehensive Planning and Implementation Project for Mental Retardation: *A Survey of Attitudes Toward Mental Retardation,* Cincinnati, 1969; Herrick, Helen: "Professional Attitudes Toward Family Attitudes," *Proceedings of the Fourth Conference on Mental Retardation,* Canadian Association on Mental Retardation, 1961, pp. 4–10; Justice, R. S., and Tjossem, T. D.: "Community Acceptance of the Retarded Child," Seattle, University of Washington School of Medicine, 1963; Dybwad, Rosemary F.: "Public Acceptance of the Mentally Retarded," excerpted as "Information Diminishes Intolerance," *Parents Voice,* National Society for the Mentally Handicapped of England, December 1966, pp. 12–14; Gatherer, A., and Reid, J. J. A.: *Public Attitudes and Mental Health Education,* England, Northamptonshire Mental Health Project, 1963; Elinson, Jack; Padilla, Elena, and Perkins, Marvin E.: *Public Image of Mental Health Services,* New York, Mental Health Materials Center, 1967; Willcocks, Arthur: "Changing Opinion—Optimism for the Future," *Mental Health,* England, National Association for Mental Health, Autumn 1967, pp. 14-16.

ses with which I began the study were as follows:

- That public awareness regarding mental retardation (including knowledge of the scientific facts and recognition of the scope of the problem) correlates with a favorable attitude.
- That the extent and nature of parent organization correlates positively with the existence of favorable public attitudes.
- That there is a relationship between public attitudes (especially attitudes of public officials) and the availability of desirable services.
- That there are differences between European and U.S. attitudes (and differences among European attitudes).
- That it is possible to modify attitudes in the direction of greater acceptance of the mentally retarded and a positive expectation.

As I visited in Europe, I found, as I had heard, that the program and prospects for the mentally retarded, particularly in the Scandinavian countries, are indeed different from what they are in the United States. And a major reason is that in those countries the attitudes are different.

Public officials, citizen leaders, journalists and professional people working with retarded children and adults all expressed attitudes and expectations which are markedly different from the prevailing views of their American counterparts.

There are three basic attitudes which I found expressed repeatedly and in many ways:

1. Mentally retarded people are human beings. They should therefore be treated with respect for their individual dignity.

2. We do not always know what capabilities a retarded person may have, but we must do all we can to help each one achieve his fullest potential.

3. It is society's responsibility to help the retarded, as it must help others who are handicapped or dependent; and society works most effectively through the state. As one Scandinavian put it, "We pay high taxes, and while we do

not enjoy it, we accept it. But we do expect that with the tax money, our government will provide for the handicapped."[3]

From these attitudes, a whole series of policies and programs flows. My visits to several countries and my interviews with knowledgeable Europeans turned up the following evidence:

1. Within the limits of each nation's resources (which are far less than ours), social services are provided as needed. Programs begin with comprehensive health services, including prevention and diagnosis. Special education services are available to all who can benefit, as they are increasingly in some of our states. For retarded adults, there are sheltered workshops, hostels for community living, and a variety of other residential facilities and programs.

2. State-operated or state-sponsored residential facilities for the retarded are small compared to state institutions in America. Sweden, for example, in 1967 had five hospitals, ranging in size from 150 to 800 beds. Additional hospitals were to be built in two "counties" (the equivalent of our states), and the national director of mental retardation programs, Karl Grunewald, said they should not be larger than 400 beds. (In the United States, many public institutions have 2,000 beds or more.) Dr. Grunewald observed, however, that most of the retarded who receive care under public auspices are in what the Swedes call "residential homes," and he emphasized that these are not at all hospital-like.

Even in the "large" Scandinavian facilities housing several hundred, the living arrangements are scaled to human proportions. The rooms are clean, light, airy, colorful, with furniture of contemporary design. The director of a public residential facility in Oslo said he knew some of his sleeping rooms were too crowded, and he hoped to be able to change

---

[3] In Norway, the national income tax ranges from 20 up to 80 percent; there is also a municipal income tax of 18 percent, and a sales tax of 12½ percent. Swedish citizens pay an average of 13 kroner ($2.60) a year for the care of the mentally retarded.

the physical arrangements in the next year or so. The largest rooms I saw there contained twelve beds; in some institutions in the United States fifty, eighty and more beds in one ward are common.

In Denmark, I visited one of the older hospitals—not the showplace that all visitors see, but one built years ago. The doctor in charge apologized that it was too large; there were 1,100 retarded persons of whom 230 were children. He said there are another 800 in the region who should receive care, but facilities are not yet available. "Why couldn't you move in a few more beds here?" I asked, comparing in my mind the generous space with the conditions I have seen in American institutions. "At least you could bring in a few more children, raise your total to 300," I suggested. "No, absolutely!" he responded. "Why not?" He had three answers: The parents would object. The staff could not work well in such conditions. "And you cannot pack children like herrings in a box."[4]

When I visited Kilkenny, Ireland, the Most Rev. Dr. Peter Birch, Bishop of Ossory, told me of his plans for a combination of hospital and school for retarded adults; he envisioned a resident population of about twenty-five. I observed that in the United States an institution of a thousand beds is considered a small one, and he replied, "Well, I have no use at all for big institutions, of any kind. I think it's an unnatural existence—and that in spite of the fact that I spent many happy years in a very big seminary when I was training for the priesthood. I still think that a small, semi-family atmosphere is more appropriate for the retarded. All these people, whether they are mildly or severely handicapped, have the faculty for affection; and it's hard to get sufficient outlet for affection in a great big institution that's bound to be impersonal."

---

[4] For additional Scandinavian perspectives on residential care, see the chapters by Nirje, Bengt; Bank-Mikkelsen, N. E., and Grunewald, Karl, in Kugel, Robert B., and Wolfensberger, Wolf: *Changing Patterns in Residential Services for the Mentally Retarded,* Washington, D.C., President's Committee on Mental Retardation, 1969.

To clarify the difference in perspectives, I remarked that in the United States, for reasons of economy, a large institution is preferable for the planner who needs to accommodate a large number of people; and considerations of affection are minor. "Yes, well," the Bishop responded, "in the United States you seem to glory in bigness anyway. But my reaction would be to try, at least, for living in a community effort. We've gone overboard on this business of great big efficiency, of big schools and all the rest. We're following your example here, in the schools, again as a question of economy and efficiency. We're gaining something, but we're also losing out. . . ."

Finally, I put one more practical question to Dr. Birch: If you were responsible for the program in Dublin (with a population of 750,000, many times the size of Kilkenny), would it be possible to establish residential facilities for the mentally retarded as small as twenty-five beds each? Would you then, I asked him, contemplate a large number of that size, or would you rather have a few larger ones—say 250 to 500 beds each? As I expected, the Bishop opted for no more than twenty-five in any facility.

3. Everywhere there is respect for privacy and individuality. Bedrooms usually had space for personal belongings, and in a hostel for young adults I visited in Copenhagen, the rooms were as varied as their occupants, with framed pictures on the wall in one, and stacks of hot-rod magazines in another.

On every tour, the director or superintendent would consistently knock before entering a room. I often asked, "Why do you knock?" The answer, usually with a surprised look, was, "It's his room. He is entitled to know I want to enter."

There were few locks. Where I observed them was on doors where crawlers or toddlers might otherwise slip out and hurt themselves. I recalled, wryly, an institution in the Pacific Northwest, where a new superintendent some years ago spent twelve thousand dollars to *remove* locks, as a way of letting his staff know that things were going to be different.

In the United States, there are still relatively few super-intendents with this point of view, but in the countries I visited it was common.

4. Inactivity for the mentally retarded in residential facilities was rare. Even quite severely handicapped individuals were encouraged to engage in some purposeful activity, often with an economic value, however meager.

5. By far the largest number of the retarded not only live in the community but participate in the community's life. A larger proportion of them work, in the European countries I heard about, than in the United States. In an economy of full employment, as exists in Denmark, retarded persons find it easier to get and hold jobs. There appeared to be little resistance; most employers just expect productivity, and if the retarded person can produce, he is employable.

6. There is a flexibility and an easy transition from one program to another. The hostel I visited in Copenhagen was for rather mildly retarded young men, but these were men who had committed crimes and had been sent by the court to an institution for the mentally retarded. When the institution staff felt that an individual could benefit from the more open and permissive atmosphere of the hostel, he was transferred. Some failed and had to go back to the institution, but some succeeded; and always there was hope and the willingness to try.

7. Throughout the Scandinavian countries, and in England as well, there is a substantial emphasis on public services. Programs for the retarded are largely under national auspices in Denmark; in Sweden, there is a partnership between the national and local authorities. In Norway, the least affluent of the three, there are cooperative arrangements between the state and voluntary agencies.

By contrast, the programs I saw in Ireland were offered under religious auspices, although also with governmental financing. In Kilkenny, for example, every good program for the mentally retarded—and I saw much that was good—derived its inspiration from the Bishop of Ossory.

There is of course more than one way to interpret a set of facts. When I offered my hypothesis to Mrs. Margaret Crozier of the National Society for Mentally Handicapped Children, in England, she commented, "It's quite the other way 'round. Attitudes have changed *because* there are good programs. For example, doctors do not any longer necessarily recommend that a retarded child be placed in an institution, because it is recognized that there are now alternatives in the community."

On the other hand, Bengt Nirje, who at that time was executive director of Sweden's Riksförbundet för Utvecklingsstörda Barn (FUB), and had visited the United States several times, told me: "There is definitely a different point of view and a different kind of philosophy when it comes to mental retardation. I think there is a much harder job that has to be done in the United States than we have. I think we have obtained a public acceptance in a higher degree than you have and an expectation of higher standards in things done— which we take for granted, but which you do not. I was very shocked by some institutions I saw, and I could see they were a result of a kind of non-thinking or non-planning."

There are three aspects in which I found the United States is ahead of the countries I visited:

In *research*, America leads the world. Albert Christensen, a successful attorney and president of Landsforeningen Evnesvages Vel, the national parents' association of Denmark, asked me, a bit wistfully, about our research programs and expressed the wish that his organization might stimulate such efforts in his own country. With limited financial resources, it is obvious that direct services must come first—although Europeans do study the findings of research in other countries and try to apply them promptly.

In *professional training*, the Europeans likewise have cause to envy us. During my twenty-one-day visit I met some highly competent and resourceful people, but it appeared that the availability of physicians, psychologists, social workers and other trained personnel was far less than ours.

The one outstandingly American way in which we excel is in the quality and extent of *voluntary citizen participation* in programs for the mentally retarded. Wherever I asked about the role of the parents and other interested citizens, the answer was either a blank look or a reference to fund-raising and public interpretation. These are of course major functions of the National Association for Retarded Children and the state and local organizations throughout the United States. Beyond these activities, however, relatives and friends of the mentally retarded in our country perform many services, direct and indirect, and contribute thousands of hours of volunteer time in institutions and community facilities.[5] An English sociologist who had worked for a time in California commented that parents of the retarded are much more actively involved in institutional care in the United States than in England.

Further, it is part of the American political reality that voluntary associations for the mentally retarded press constantly for improvement and expansion of existing programs. In Sweden, Richard Sterner, President of the FUB, told me, this is an important function of his group, but in the other countries the public officials seemed to take the lead, and the citizen organizations had a different role.

We in the United States have much to learn about creative provision of needed services for the mentally retarded. We can learn from the countries of Europe, if we wish to. And with our resources, we can lead the world in making it possible for retarded people to reach their full potential as participating members of our society.

---

[5] Sills, David L.: *The Volunteers*. Glencoe, Illinois, The Free Press, 1957. See especially Chapter IV, "Assisting Polio Victims," for a description of the range of volunteer activities which typify the American system.

Chapter Two

CONCERN FOR THE HANDICAPPED: AN INSIGHT FROM SWEDEN

WHEN ALL the motorists in Sweden successfully switched over to driving on the right side of the road one Sunday morning in September 1967, the event was a triumph of careful planning and effective organization. It was also one more example of Scandinavian concern for the handicapped members of society.

The changeover, which put Sweden in step with all the other countries in continental Europe, received worldwide public notice, under such headlines as "Massive Motoring Migraine: Sweden Shifts to the Right" (*San Francisco Chronicle*) and "Sweden's Move to the Right Called A Success—But 8,197 are Charged with Speeding" (*International Herald Tribune*).

What was not so well known, outside of Sweden itself, was the concern for the safety of children, elderly persons and the handicapped, and the thoroughness with which preparations were made to protect these special groups of the population.

It was my good fortune to visit Stockholm just three weeks after Dagen H—H Day, or Right-Hand Day. I called on Högertraffikkommissioner Lars Skjöld, who was responsible for directing the nationwide effort that prepared Sweden's drivers of automobiles, bicycles and mopeds. The change was accomplished within a few minutes around 5 A.M. Sunday, September 3, 1967, but Mr. Skjöld told me it was the culmination of four years of planning and preparation.

It was a masterpiece of organization and execution, involving the redesign and rebuilding of vehicles, streets and highways; the revising of street signs by the thousands; temporary lowering of the speed limits; the mobilizing of law-enforcement officers throughout the nation; and special measures to alert shut-ins, tourists, foreign-speaking members of the population and other special groups.

Not a single medium of communication was overlooked in the campaign—from press, radio and television, to conferences and speaking engagements, to brochures and posters in ten languages. *Everyone* got the message, and "everyone" specifically included the blind, the deaf, the crippled and the mentally retarded.

In fact, the blind, the deaf, the crippled and the retarded were the object of a special phase of the information campaign; a specialist devoted his energies exclusively to the problems of communicating with the handicapped and their families. He was Anders Arnör, an employee of the Association for the Blind, who was made available on a half-time basis to work on the special problems of the handicapped in connection with the changeover to right-hand driving.

"But why so much special effort?" I asked Mr. Skjöld, and later Mr. Arnör. "Surely the blind do not drive in Sweden—and probably there are not so many crippled or mentally retarded drivers that they required all this special attention?"

The answer illuminated the thinking of the Swedes. "No, the blind, the crippled and the mentally retarded do not drive—but they are affected by driving. They are passengers . . . they are pedestrians . . . they are part of the world around the driver . . . they are part of our society. And so we had to make sure that their safety too was insured."

Mr. Arnör's task had three aspects:

1. To adapt the general information for people who could not see, who could not hear, or who could not understand. This meant taking the great mass of materials being produced—the news articles, the brochures, the posters, the

radio and television announcements, the films—and redesigning them so they would have meaning for people with diverse physical and mental handicaps.

2. To develop and transmit tips for the crippled on how to get out of cars. Just as drivers would have to overcome lifelong patterns of steering, parking, signaling and stopping, the passengers must likewise be alert to the changed situation created by right-hand driving, particularly when alighting from vehicles. For those with physical disabilities, the retraining took on special complications.

3. To provide information to the public about the handicapped and their special needs in relation to the changes in driving patterns. It was not enough for motorists (and bicyclists) to learn to drive safely and cautiously in the new situation; they must also be alert to those around them who might not be fully aware of the changed situation. These would include young children, some elderly persons, and many of the blind, the deaf and the mentally retarded.

How did Mr. Skjöld and his staff, and more particularly Mr. Arnör, go about their task?

Mr. Skjöld had a staff of fifty persons directly responsible to him, plus hundreds of other government employees throughout the country who were working on the tasks associated with the changeover. When I asked him what was the most important single thing which produced the success of the right-hand change, he quickly replied: "Everything. The engineering tasks, the role of the police, the information effort all were essential, and without all of these elements we could not have succeeded."

Then he thought a while, and added: "If anything was most important, it was kindness...the consideration which each person had for the others on the first day."

The handicapped presented special problems. The blind could not read the brochures; the deaf could not hear the radio announcements; and the mentally retarded, whose understanding was limited, presented in some ways the most difficult problems of communication.

For the blind, Mr. Arnör developed special materials in Braille, as well as relying heavily on radio and other ear-oriented channels. For the deaf and the crippled, more varied avenues of communication were available.

To reach the mentally retarded and prepare them for the change in traffic patterns was a more difficult task. As Mr. Arnör commented, it takes much time and repetition to train people so that they can go safely on the streets, even in such a simple routine as walking from home to bus. It was not feasible to start ahead of time to prepare the retarded for the driving change to come, because they might begin to apply their new learning, with regard to the right-hand driving, while motorists were still driving on the left. This phase of the campaign, then, had to be different from the nationwide effort directed at the main body of the population.

The decision was made to communicate largely through the parents of the mentally retarded, although there were also messages directed to teachers, workshop directors and other persons working with the retarded. Meetings, publications and specially prepared television programs were principal avenues of communication utilized for this purpose.

Perhaps the most important single element in protecting the mentally retarded from harmful effects of the changeover was the close cooperation between the Swedish government and the FUB, the Riksförbundet för Utvecklingsstörda Barn, or nationwide association for retarded children.

There were discussions with leaders of the national organization and meetings of local parent groups, at which speakers presented the plans for the changeover to the right-hand driving and explained what this would mean for the the mentally retarded. There were also instructions on how to prepare retarded children and adults for the change. Similar discussions were held with operators of homes for the retarded, so that they too might prepare the handicapped residents of their facilities for Dagen H.

The Swedish government and the FUB cooperated in the production and wide distribution of a special issue of *FUB-Kontakt*, the magazine of the national association. In twenty-four pages of articles and pictures, the publication described the impending change to right-hand driving, indicated how this would affect the mentally retarded, and spelled out what parents and other adults responsible for the retarded should do to prepare them for the new traffic pattern. The special articles on every aspect of the change were supplemented by photographs and color reproductions of the various street signs. The pictures showed a young retarded boy, aided by an adult, waiting to cross the street, pushing a button to change the traffic signal, and otherwise conducting himself properly and with safety.

One article, by a professor from the University of Uppsala, spelled out what the children must learn to do and how to train them for the coming change, and the author adjured the parents, "Your children must learn the new behavior patterns so that they do the right thing automatically."

The materials were published in mid-May. Then there were meetings, in every county of Sweden, both for parents and for the operators of homes for the retarded. In addition to giving instructions and distributing the printed materials, the authorities allowed opportunity for questions and discussion.

The special edition of *FUB-Kontakt*, though a basic document, was only one of the many pieces of printed material made available to families of the retarded. Mr. Arnör remarked, as I had already observed, that the volume and distribution of information was so massive that, as he put it, "Everyone must come in contact with it." So the parents of the retarded were already fully aware, simply as residents of Sweden during the big informational campaign, of what was in store; in addition, then, they were given special materials for the guidance and instruction of their handicapped youngsters. The brightly colored and illustrated pamphlet, "Children in Right-Hand Traffic," was made available and was interpreted for parents, including those whose retarded relatives were adult. This publication was also distributed to schools, day centers and other services for retarded people.

To reach the retarded children and adolescents themselves, the authorities developed special material for use on popular established television programs. For the parents, there were special programs—a half-hour on radio and a quarter-hour on television—during the week preceding H Day. The broadcasts, in turn, were intensively promoted by means of printed schedules which were distributed to the parents. The fact that Sweden has one television channel and three radio stations serving the entire country helped insure what American advertising executives would describe as "saturation."

For his third major task—informing the public about the problems of the handicapped—Mr. Arnör again turned to the broadcast media. There were "spot announcements" on radio, repeated many times a day, starting in March and continuing until September. There were spots on television, strategically placed after the news at 7:30 P.M.—in what American broadcasters and advertisers would call "prime time." There were also two special TV shows used during the week before the changeover. Each of these was broadcast three times: in the afternoon, evening and late at night.

Now that the campaign is over, I asked Mr. Arnör, do you think of anything you might have done better? "Yes," he replied. "We should have given more instructions to the whole staffs of the homes for the retarded, not only to the operators. It's true they all knew about the Högertraffik, but they did not know how to teach the retarded about the change. This we would do differently." Also, one worker with the retarded had suggested a printed card, small enough to carry in the pocket, with simple instructions on how to conduct oneself on the street and in traffic. This suggestion came too late to be put into effect, but Mr. Arnör thought it was a good idea.

The pragmatic American must, finally, ask Did it work?

Mr. Arnör's response: "I have not heard of any accidents with the retarded."

In all of Sweden, he told me, there was only one accident involving a handicapped person. A deaf woman, crossing the street to catch a bus, looked the wrong way. She did not hear the oncoming traffic, and she was hit. No other mishaps; not a single retarded person injured.

What does the changeover in a European nation's driving patterns mean in terms of our concern for persons who are handicapped? It seems to me there are several items of significance in Sweden's experience with the Högertraffik effort:

1. The project was successful. This tells us that, no matter how massive and how drastic a change society seeks to make, it can work. In a life-or-death matter involving all the people of a nation, there can be success. The principal element in Sweden's effort was thorough preparation, starting far in advance.

2. Behavior *can* be changed. This is a tremendously significant finding.

3. There was, as there had to be, special attention to the handicapped; and the attention manifested itself in great care and preparation. Mr. Skjöld and his colleagues in traffic safety reflected the nation's attitude toward handicapped and dependent people. They respected the mentally retarded (and other handicapped individuals) as human beings, and they gave the special protective services these people required. The concern for human lives and safety did not discriminate as to the relative worthiness of the citizens of Sweden.

Chapter Three

THE MOTHER WHO COPES

IN A UNIVERSITY TOWN about an hour's railroad ride from London, there lives a young family. Most of the week, because the husband is a lorry driver who is frequently on the road, the family consists of the wife and five children. When I visited them, the children's ages ranged from eight to two.

The family lives in a Council flat—a low-rent, publicly subsidized apartment. The project is not as massive, dreary and deteriorating as some public housing in the United States, but it is plain, spartan and unadorned.

Four of the children are boys. One has a hearing impairment, and another has shown increasing symptoms of emotional disturbance. The daughter, five years old when I visited, was severely mentally retarded and physically handicapped.

What does a mother in such circumstances do? How does she manage her life? In the words of the person who took me to visit the woman, "She copes."

There could, of course, be such a family in the United States: living in public housing; the husband away much of the time at a steady but low-paying job; several small children, close in age, with diverse handicapping conditions traceable to a variety of causes.

Is there any difference? Is there anything distinctive about the English family's life style or social resources that facilitates survival?

Undoubtedly the most important thing is the character and strength of the mother. In any country, in any environment, she would be unusual. She loves and ministers to her children, including the retarded daughter, with an intensity,

21

a determination and a resignation that are wondrous to observe. Of limited education but unlimited tenacity, she accepts the bureaucratic procedures of health professionals and public officials alike, yet she continues to seek for her little girl the help she feels must exist for the child.

The little girl cannot feed or dress herself; she is getting heavier; she bites and she pulls your hair in frustration; she is increasingly harder to manage, and she is dependent on her mother for everything. The neighbors look on the child as one of the family, yet the mother can never get anyone to look after her—even grandmother—because they are fearful of an accident with the essentially helpless youngster.

To the child's age of five, the mother has still not had an intelligible diagnosis. One doctor, years ago, used "a long word beginning with H." Months later, in another clinic, a different doctor helped her recall: "hydrocephalus." (This later turned out to be the wrong diagnosis.) When the child was one year old, a doctor predicted that at age seven she would have the mental capabilities of a two-year-old; already, the mother observes, this has proved untrue.

When she asks the general medical practitioner for additional information, or tests, or for referral to a specialist, he takes offense and says that if she does not trust him perhaps she should get another doctor. This is possible under Britain's National Health Service, but it is not easy. In the community where this family lives (which is not necessarily typical), it is hard to get to see a doctor, even in cases of genuine medical emergency; and at best, the doctor has time for only a quick examination and prescription, never for the interpretation and counseling which would make so much difference in the mother's life and in the child's.

The mother could get the specialized, competent, understanding medical care and counseling she needs for her retarded child; but she would have to go to a private physician. This is out of the question, for financial reasons. So she continues to seek, and to ask, and to cope.

Nevertheless, the family does have some protection and

assurances. There is a basic health system, under public auspices, and whatever its inadequacies the mother knows it is available without financial burden. There are training centers, from preschool through adulthood, and while they have their limitations and often their waiting lists, the prospects for the future point toward growth and improvement of programs for handicapped individuals. And finally, there are nationally guaranteed public assistance programs, so that the family with the handicapped child need never agonize under the extra burden of extreme poverty.

Withal, life for a lower middle class family with a severely handicapped child in England is not all that different from what it would be in a comparable college town in the United States. The significant difference, to the extent there is one, lies in the nascent attitude of acceptance of social responsibility for individual problems, as expressed in Britain's welfare and socialized health system.

Chapter Four

ROLE OF THE PARENT
ORGANIZATIONS

ALTHOUGH the primary focus of my study was on attitudes, rather than on the state of organization, I looked also at the strength and the role of the parent organizations in a number of countries of Europe.

In fact, in the series of hypotheses I formulated in advance of my trip,[1] I had suggested that the extent and nature of parent organization correlated with favorable public attitudes on mental retardation.

The former editor of *Australian Children Limited*, J.D. Van Pelt, who received a Rosemary Dybwad Award from NARC to study parent organization in the United States about the same time I was visiting Europe, reacted to my outline with these comments:

"Numbering your theses I-V, I agree that:

"Public awareness can be roused (V), amongst others by parent organizations (II).

"This will result in favourable public attitudes (I).

"This, in turn, will lead to more and better services."

Now I do not agree entirely with Mr. Van Pelt's observations, though they may be appropriate in the Australian context, but I cite his remarks to indicate something of the frame of mind with which I approached my European study. I found a situation quite different from what I expected.

---

[1] See page 7.

To begin with, I found that in some of the countries the national organizations were not composed primarily of parents and friends of the mentally retarded, as in the United States, but of persons as well whose primary interests were in other areas. In fact, some of the national organizations had no individual members at all, but rather were federations of organizations established for other purposes, loosely affiliated because of their concern for the mentally retarded.

The National Association for the Mentally Handicapped of Ireland, for example, lists "affiliated organizations" to the number of sixty-six. The alphabetical listing starts with Association of Parents and Friends of Mentally Handicapped Children, to be sure, but it ends with Workers' Union of Ireland. In between, in addition to parent organizations, there are professional organizations (Irish Medical Association, Irish National Teachers' Association, Irish Nurses Organization), religious orders (Brothers of Charity, Galway; Sisters of La Sagesse, Sligo), service groups (Cork Lions Clubs, Soroptimist Club of Drogheda) and the Protestant Child Care Association.

The honorary secretary of the NAMHI, Lieut. Col. Joseph Adams, told me: "We don't go in for parent associations as such. We have mixed associations—parents and friends. We think that it's a bad association that entirely consists of one interest or one discipline. We think that it is a far better balance to have an association where parents, or doctors, or psychologists, or anybody else interested in the field, can work in one group. Then you get an idea of what the problem is from all sides." In the past, he told me, one chairman of NAMHI has been a parent, another a doctor, and it could be a psychologist, "or even a trade unionist."

The National Association in Ireland has no paid staff; all the officers are voluntary. Col. Adams himself is a professional soldier and, as others of his age, he is encouraged to do voluntary social service.

"We're purely an amateur body, and naturally we're not as efficient as a paid professional group would be," he said. It seemed to me the tenor of the comment was rueful rather than apologetic. There was a note of pride, however, as he added: "Nevertheless, we get quite a bit done by devoting our time to it. There is still a great love of humanity among the Irish, and they don't look for a dollar for service, if you know what I mean."

Another point to be made about the state of organization in the countries of Europe is the *internationality* of the continent. There is a considerable sensitivity, in each of the countries, to what is going on elsewhere. It is commonplace, for example, for "Scandinavian" conferences to be held, rather than only meetings of Swedes, Danes or Norwegians, and the proceedings or other resulting publications are usually available in several languages, often including English.

When I talked in Copenhagen with Albert Christensen, the president of Landsforeningen Evnesvages Vel, the organization of Denmark, he thoughtfully offered me a copy of a letter he had recently written about his organization to officials of UNAPEI, the French national association. Routinely, he had made copies of the letter in French and in Danish.

Another example of the extent of interest in the international exchange of ideas and materials is the *Newsletter* of the International League of Societies for the Mentally Handicapped. In fact, the existence and the flourishing activity of the International League is an attribute of European patterns which is quite different from prevalent American attitudes. The *Newsletter* is currently published from Waltham, Massachusetts, where the editor, Rosemary F. Dybwad, now works, but the publication continues to reflect worldwide contributions and readership.

Even where the parent and citizen associations for the mentally handicapped were well organized, it struck me that their roles were primarily fund-raising, to some extent the promotion of public awareness, and of course the provision of mutual solace and information among the parents. Almost nowhere did I find an active involvement in volunteer services for the mentally retarded; and the function of social action (or political pressure) was present in only a limited way in some of the countries.

In Oslo, it is true, the whole Støttelaget for Åndssvake is in a way the elongated shadow of one devoted parent, Mrs. Ragnhild Schibbye; it may well be that one would find this pattern elsewhere in Norway. In Denmark, however, as I visited various state institutions and facilities for the mentally retarded and admired the programs and the high staff ratios, when I asked about a role for volunteers, the reaction was generally negative. Even the thought that parents of the residents might visit regularly and perform some services for their own children (and others) drew a cautious and at times suspicious response. I found the same atmosphere as I visited St. Augustine's in Blackrock, Ireland, where the devoted Brothers of St. John of God provide a warm and sheltering atmosphere for the mildly and moderately retarded. While parents are allowed to visit, and some do more or less frequently, there is apparently no role for them or other volunteers in the program itself.

As to the "pressure" role of the organized parents, I found it at its most active in Sweden. Richard Sterner, president of the Swedish FUB, told me there is an important role for the parent organization, despite the dominance of the public sector and the commitment of all political parties to the provision of social welfare programs. His organization, Dr. Sterner said, must provide the expertise, the knowledge as to what services are required and what methods are best, and to work with Members of Parliament on the provisions of legislation. (The local associations, he added, perform similar functions on their level.) The FUB has some influence, he said, and is working to make it stronger. "We've got to press all the time. Otherwise, they won't do enough, and they will do some things in the wrong manner." Dr. Sterner was not talking of the administrative officials, under the direction of Karl Grunewald, with whom the FUB has a cooperative and highly effective working relationship, but rather of the political leaders, in Parliament and in the government, who are less familiar and less concerned with the problems of mental retardation.

The sophistication of the Swedish FUB did not, however, find counterparts in the other countries I visited.

Following, in somewhat more detail, are impressions I gathered during my brief visits to the five countries, and from correspondence and supplementary conversations elsewhere.

Ireland

The state of parent (or citizen) organization appeared quite primitive, resembling the situation in the United States in the early 1950's. A knowledgeable and sensitive Irishman, who had spent some years in the United States, suggested to me that the initiative lies largely with religious leaders; and my observations in Blackrock and Kilkenny bore this out. Government's role is limited, for the most part, to financial assistance, and the sponsorship and operation of programs is largely in the hands of the religious. In my discussions with parents and others, I noted an unfailing deference to the religious and professional people.

Kilkenny is a small town, some seventy-five miles from Dublin. It is perhaps typical of the communities of Ireland, except in one respect: the vision and forceful leadership of the Bishop of Ossory has transformed the plight of the mentally retarded and their families into a situation of hope. It was my privilege, on the evening of an all-day visit to Kilkenny, to address the Kilkenny Association of Parents and Friends of Mentally Handicapped Children. This was only the fourth meeting of the organization, which had come into existence the previous spring, and the parents, teachers, clergymen and others in the audience were hungry for information and for guidance. There was intense interest in the state and focus of organizational activities in the United States and perhaps a sense of helplessness for the new local organization as compared with what the audience saw as the affluent and powerful NARC in America. I explained that as effective as NARC is on the national scene, the parents who meet in

Yakima, Washington, or Fort Bragg, California, face (or have faced) the same problems as those in Kilkenny, Ireland.

England

Other than reports of the President's Panel on Mental Retardation and other Americans who had visited Europe, the first material which came to hand as I prepared for my study was a packet of periodicals of the National Society for the Mentally Handicapped of England. These provided a window on the state of organization and the attitudes of the parents themselves. The tone of the publications was both hortatory and hopeful, resembling the newsletters of local associations in the United States. Emphasis was on the need for funds, for understanding and for "sympathy." Although there was reference to "a great national movement," the focus seemed to be on local objectives and local programs. Interestingly, in view of the clash of attitudes in the United States, between the NARC position and the activities of some local units, an editorial in the English *Parents' Voice* advocated that the organization demonstrate needed services, then obtain them from other sources, rather than attempting to provide directly for all the retarded.

Although I was unable to meet the editor of this stimulating magazine, Mrs. Judy Fryd, I did receive a long, thoughtful letter from her. Commenting on the pamphlet NSMHC had recently published under the title "Stress in Families with Mentally Handicapped Children," Mrs. Fryd observed:

> It is excellent as far as it goes, but it deals almost exclusively with the *negative* side of the problem, i.e. the parents' difficulties. It does not describe the ways in which parents cope with their problems and try to canalise their grief and disappointment and anger into socially valuable action, e.g. the original founding of the NSMHC itself—as the Association of Parents of Backward Children in this country, the NARC in USA and other similar societies in various other countries. At local level, the parents have not been content to accept the lowly role to which they and their children were consigned but

have got together to provide a happy social life among friends
who were in the same boat; to lobby the local authorities for
a share of the community expenditure on education and
health services and recreational facilities (towards which
parents of these children pay the same rates as those with
normal children); and to raise funds from their local communities to provide facilities such as clubrooms, minibuses,
centers for nursery schooling and junior and adult training in
advance of public provision; and to provide additional comforts
and amenities for patients in State Hospitals for the mentally
handicapped. They have also raised funds for research into the
causes, treatment and educational methods and creation of
therapeutic environments, through the National Society's research and project funds.

One cannot talk about parents' "stress" without taking into
account all these things the parents have done to help themselves and their children. Nevertheless, when all that has been
done, by the Society and by the Government and Local
Authorities is taken into consideration, it still remains a tragic
blow when partners find they have borne such an afflicted child,
and perhaps the most important side of our work is helping
parents to share their sorrow and learn to find joy in the
simple achievements of children of limited ability. They can
learn from the experiences of their parents, realize that it
IS possible to "get over it" to the extent of being able to live full
and happy family lives within the scope of the child's limitations
and needs.

I have quoted at such length because I consider Mrs.
Fryd's letter quite revealing, not only its description of what
the parents and their organization have accomplished in recent
years, but as much for what it discloses of her own attitudes,
as an articulate leader of the movement.

While in London, I had the opportunity for an extended
interview with an English sociologist who had recently spent
a year in the United States and who was therefore able to
offer some insightful observations by way of comparison between the two countries. While her professional interest was
not directly in mental retardation, she had had the opportunity to observe institutions and parent-organization activities in both countries.

It was her observation that in the United States the

parents are "more involved, more demanding, more active." In England, she said, the parents merely join the organization and pay their dues. She reported little use made of volunteers in the English institutions—rather, a resentment and resistance on the part of staff members. The English parents do spend a good deal of time collecting money; they arrange, and pay for, outings for the children; they send Christmas cards and birthday cards for the children who have no one of their own; and occasionally they visit—nothing more.

One explanation offered by the sociologist was that the atmosphere is more authoritarian in England than in the United States. The people in charge feel that they are *completely* in charge, she told me, and there is an active effort to discourage volunteer service. Another factor is the prevalent English view that doctors are "superior beings" and not to be questioned. And, she added, "it's also a class thing. The middle class, in America, make more demands than the parents of the mentally handicapped in England."

In Oxford, I had a group interview with four city officials, The substance of their remarks may have been influenced by the fact that the conference had been arranged by a local citizen, an intelligent and articulate parent, who sat in on the discussion. Between the lines of what was actually said, however, I discerned a bewilderment at the fact that I had even asked the question about volunteers.

The first reaction of one of the men, the manager of an industrial training center for retarded youths and adults, was vigorously negative. The thought that volunteers might be useful in reducing the demands on him and his staff appeared to him as a threat; he feared that if the authorities saw that he could make do with unpaid personnel, he would lose part of his already insufficient staff. The supervisor of the training center for moderately to severely retarded youngsters, however, thought a moment and commented, "It would be helpful to have someone take the children on outings. Then people in the community could see that they do behave properly." As I pursued the question, all agreed that there was a public-education benefit to volunteer involvement. Another member of the group commented that students do work at the retardation center, but there are no housewives or others from the neighborhood. The volunteers, it appeared, are mostly young people who are considering their own career directions.

What struck me about the responses to my question was the fact that there seemed to be no consensus, nor even shared thinking, among the Oxford city officials. Their reactions were largely negative at first; then, as they thought about it, they recalled examples of volunteer service in their own programs and began to acknowledge the values and benefits. It was rather astonishing that they apparently had not thought it out before; that is, they did not seem to have a philosophy regarding the use and role of volunteers.

Denmark

With direction of programs highly centralized in (national) governmental hands, the role of a parent or citizen organization is correspondingly limited. Nevertheless, officials of the National Service for the Mentally Retarded attributed to the parents' organization a most important development of recent years: a change in the attitudes of parents themselves. They used to be ashamed of the fact that they had retarded children, I was told, but this is no longer the case. The national organization has utilized the mass media of communication, notably radio and television, to talk frankly about retardation, to bring the subject into the open, and to encourage the parents to speak up for their children. The result has not only been a growing atmosphere of public acceptance, but a changed attitude on the part of those who have experienced retardation in their own families.

Landsforeningen Evnesvages Vel performs another function, in cooperation with the public agency. Because capital funds are not readily available from public sources, the parents' organization will buy a house, and the state will then rent it for use as a hostel or some other institutional use for the retarded. The government then controls the program which is conducted in the building. The voluntary organization is thus a landlord-partner in the provision of services for the mentally retarded.[2] Other than this, the principal functions described for me by N. E. Bank-Mikkelsen, director of the Danish National Service for the Mentally Retarded, were to bring parents together, to help them understand their own problem, to do public relations, and to collect money. Albert Christensen, Copenhagen barrister and dynamic president of the national association, saw the organization's responsibilities in essentially the same terms. He put fund-raising first, and showed me a paper flower (*forglem-mig-ej*, the forget-me-not) which is the souvenir device used for the annual solicitation. He also told me of how his organization a few weeks before my visit had taken over Copenhagen's famous Strøget, or Walking Street, for a display of paintings, handicrafts and other articles fashioned by the retarded. As a result of the fact that thousands of strollers saw the displays, Mr. Christensen told me, there was already a noticeable change in public attitudes. Moreover, he said, business was now booming at the shop maintained by the organization.

In a lengthy letter to the director-general of UNAPEI, the French national organization of parents, which he had written just a few weeks before my visit, Mr. Christensen emphasized the primary function of the Danish organization as spreading awareness and improving understanding of mental retardation. He described the active public-information program and indicated that his group works in close cooperation with the state, which has the major service role. He placed considerable emphasis on research and indicated that some of the funds raised go for this purpose.

---

[2] Interestingly, there is a similar partnership between government and parent organization—though with different roles—in the establishment and operation of hostels for the retarded in New York State. Under legislation enacted in 1967 and currently being implemented, the State Department of Mental Hygiene may purchase or lease land, renovate or construct a building and turn it over to a voluntary organization to operate as a residential facility for retarded adults. The State pays half the cost of operation, and the organization finances the remainder through fees or philanthropic contributions.

A member of Mr. Bank-Mikkelsen's staff raised the possibility of still another service which might be performed by the association. "It's not a tradition in this country to do things yourself when the state pays for everything," she said, "but we are suggesting to the parents' organization that it take responsibility for guardianship."[3]

Sweden

Riksförbundet för Utvecklingsstörda Barn (FUB), the Swedish national organization of parents and friends of the mentally handicapped, seemed to me the strongest and most effective organization of its kind that I encountered in Europe.

At a session of the Congress of the International Association for the Scientific Study of Mental Deficiency, at Montpellier, the FUB president, Richard Sterner, commented on the prepared papers with the observation that in Sweden the main function of the parents is to exert pressure on the government. He elaborated by emphasizing the importance of public opinion and the value of publicity. Later, in conversation with me, he made it clear that he sees these as closely related means and ends.

In Sweden, he told me, the retarded are considered as other handicapped persons, in that the problems are similar and the solutions come from the same source.[4] Recognition of the retarded as one group of the handicapped, however, he

---

[3] Conversely, in California at the same time, parents and others concerned about long-term protective services for the mentally retarded were developing legislative proposals under which the State would take responsibility for the provision of guardianship of the person as well as the estate. In other states there have been diverse proposals, but most of them call for legislative (that is to say, official public) action.

[4] In New York City, Mayor John V. Lindsay took two separate actions early in 1968. He established the Office of Mental Retardation, and he appointed the Mayor's Advisory Committee on the Handicapped. For almost two years there was virtually no communication between the two. Then, early in 1970, the Mayor asked the City's director of mental retardation services to provide staff services to the Advisory Committee, and there began to be an exchange of ideas and a joining of efforts as between the needs of the mentally and the physically handicapped. This New York City development, however, is not typical of the United States.

said was relatively recent and was due in part to the emergence of the parent association which started in the early 1950's.

"We consider charity and fund-raising undignified," he said, "Everything ought to be provided by the state and by local government, and financed by taxes." This was perhaps the clearest and most succinct expression of the Scandinavian point of view I was to hear during my study; and the most direct example of the difference from the American attitude.

In spite of his derogatory comment about fund-raising, however, Dr. Sterner said FUB does engage in such activity, because as he put it, "there is a long distance between what has been achieved and what should be there." He said FUB concentrates on certain pioneer projects, in order to show the public authorities what can be done. Having demonstrated both the need and the practicality, FUB then presses the public sector to take over first the financing and then the operation of the program; "and then we move on to something else."

Bengt Nirje, FUB's executive director, was extremely well informed on the economic, sociological and political attributes of his society. He comprehends the social philosophy of his nation and his time. His insight was undoubtedly one reason for the effectiveness of the FUB.

Although he expressed the same attitude toward fund-raising as Dr. Sterner, the executive director told me of FUB's first fund-raising effort on a national scale, in which it raised 500,000 kroner ($100,000). The proceeds went into a foundation for sheltered workshops and multi-disciplinary research, in cooperation with the County of Uppsala and the University of Uppsala. He emphasized that this is a demonstration and expressed confidence that the government will eventually take responsibility. Local units of the national FUB had already accomplished similar results with the establishment of day centers, preschools, play schools, occupational centers and sheltered workshops.

In addition to pressure by demonstration, FUB was actively involved in developing and promoting passage of a bill which would extend the government's role in provision of services for the mentally retarded. One of the areas of concern at the time of my visit was education for retarded adults.

Mr. Nirje described the philosophy of the FUB. ("We didn't know we had a philosophy in Scandinavia," he told me with a smile, "until a few years back, when people from other countries came to look and we had to explain what we were doing.") FUB's aim, he said, is "to create a situation of life for the mentally retarded which is as close to normal as possible."[5] The examples he gave were vivid, homely and apt.

There are two groups of parents, Mr. Nirje explained: the older ones, who had received no advice and who learned to cope with the problems by themselves; and the young ones, who are better prepared and less shocked when they learn they have a retarded child.

But why do parents join the association, I asked, if they now get all these services as a right? They join, Mr. Nirje responded, because when they go to the doctor, or to the school, or to any other place of information or service, the person in charge tells them about FUB, and they discover that through the organization they can meet other parents with the same kind of problems. Moverover, the local societies have leisure-time activities, summer camps, study courses for parents, and other direct services.

"We think there are three things of importance in the parents' association," Mr. Nirje said: "One, to have a pleasant atmosphere in our local societies. In locals where there is aggressiveness and conflict, it is bad because it creates an additional burden for the families. Two, the economic

---

[5] Mr. Nirje has since developed his concept of "normalization" further. See his contribution, "The Normalization Principle and Its Human Management Implications," in Kugel, Robert B., and Wolfensberger, Wolf: *Changing Patterns in Residential Services for the Mentally Retarded,* Washington, D.C., President's Committee on Mental Retardation, 1969.

situation of parents is important. That doesn't mean we are there to provide money—but it means that we have to push to obtain services. Three, parents who are informed, who have studied, who know the facts, are better able to handle the situation; so our job is to give information."

With all of the activity and success, Mr. Nirje said FUB has a long way to go. At the time of my visit it had 10,000 members, out of a population of eight million. He estimated there are 75,000 to 100,000 retarded persons in Sweden, and instead of 6,000 families represented in FUB, he expressed the view that the membership should represent at least 25,000.

When I got to Stockholm, the FUB claims and concerns were confirmed for me by Karl Grunewald, who is in charge of mental retardation services for the Swedish government, as an official of the Ministry of Social Affairs. In addition to his responsibilities for planning and developing programs, Dr. Grunewald functions as an Ombudsman, which means that he maintains continuing surveillance of state and county programs and protects the interests of the retarded and their families.

The parents' organization in the last ten years, Dr. Grunewald told me, has taken the mentally retarded from anonymity. He cited photographs in the newspapers as one example; such public notice had never occurred before FUB began.[6] On the county level, the organization functioned as a pressure group, he said, and then the county officials came to him. On the national level, the FUB executive director and president came directly to him. If there was trouble at the county level (where the services are provided), Nirje and Grunewald typically went together to investigate, to meet with the county officials and with the county parent organizations. The law specifies, Dr. Grunewald told me, that

---

[6] For a description of how the press looks at mental retardation in the Scandinavian countries, see Chapter 7, "Attitudes of the Media." For an American contrast, see Chapter 10, "What Is a Handicap?," especially pp. 75–76.

the board for the mentally retarded at the county level must cooperate with the parents' association.

Dr. Grunewald's only complaint about FUB is that it calls itself, and operates, as an organization of parents of retarded children. He does not feel a similar pressure for older people who are retarded, and he regrets this. He thinks the association should change its name and affirm its interest in all the mentally retarded.[7] From my conversations with Bengt Nirje and others, I suspected that the situation was changing and Dr. Grunewald would soon get his wish.

My observation, from talking with representatives of the state and the parents' organization, is that working relationships are quite close. There is mutual respect, and a recognition of the need for each other.

Norway

The most substantial activity of the parents in Norway appears to be in the provision of direct services at the local level. In Oslo, I visited the widely known Ragna Ringdals Daghjem, which serves mentally retarded persons across a wide range of handicaps and age levels, and with a variety of programs from day activity to residential care. There is a close working relationship between the organization and the government, so intricate that the physician director could not answer categorically when I asked whether he was a public employee. He explained that his employer is the parents' organization, but his salary is paid by the National Department of Social Welfare and by the City of Oslo.

Mrs. Ragnhild Schibbye, leader of the Oslo organization for some thirty years, told me it had 968 members in 1966, but she could not say how many were parents. The organization raises funds by bazaars, a lottery and contributions. It also has a major planning role, Mrs. Schibbye said, whereas the state and the city provide the funds.

---

[7] The Canadian Association for Retarded Children changed its name, in 1968, to Canadian Association for the Mentally Retarded. In the United States, NARC still retains its original name, but some of the state and local associations have made the change.

The national organization had been established quite recently. A major activity at the time of my visit was the sponsorship of *Hjerte Bladet*,[8] a compact magazine with a regular circulation of some 3,000. A special issue published in June 1967, however, included several articles defining broad program objectives, and it went to 20,000 persons, including members of Parliament and leaders of the nation's press.

Germany

At Montpellier, Tom Mutters talked with me about Lebenshilfe für das Geistig Behinderte Kind (LGBK), the German association for the retarded. Both the national organization and the local units include parents and professional people, in about 50-50 proportions. There are 280 local associations and eleven state associations.

Parents, professionals and representatives of the local authorities serve together on the local board, with no essential conflict of interest. During the Congress of the International Association for the Scientific Study of Mental Deficiency, there was a dispute over organizational representation. Whereas the distinction between the National Association for Retarded Children and the American Association on Mental Deficiency in the United States is clear, despite some overlapping of membership, the composition of LGBK and some of the other national organizations in Europe raised questions as to the appropriate representation in the International Association, which aims to be the professional group, and the International League of Societies for the Mentally Handicapped, the world organization of parents' associations.

The local associations in Germany run the programs, Mr. Mutters told me. The schools have become public, but the day care programs, workshops and hostels remain under private sponsorship. The local authorities pay the sponsor for the program, collecting what they can from the parents.

---

[8] For an example of how an ingenuous American visitor's observations found their way into the pages of *Hjerte Bladet,* see Chapter 7, "Attitudes of the Media," especially pp. 61–62.

The national association has a service for newspapers, and the press uses the material, Mr. Mutters said. There is also a television program aired every six weeks which offers information, entertainment and a lottery. With a population in West Germany of 55 million, the association has 30,000 members. The members of LGBK do not identify, however, with the parents of the mildly retarded, who come mostly from the lower classes, Mr. Mutters told me.

The parents' organization was set up from the top, at the national level, and Mr. Mutters said he personally worked in the communities to establish each local association.

In East Germany, he said, there is nothing. It is impossible to set up a citizen organization, he explained, because the state is responsible for all programs. (I was later to recall this comment and to compare Mr. Mutters' evaluation with my observations in Sweden, where the state's role is major but the parents' organization is so influential. But perhaps Mr. Mutters' afterthought holds the explanation. "Eastern Germany," he said, "is the most Communistic country in Europe.")

Spain

In a brief conversation at Montpellier, Jesus Avantos of Barcelona informed me that the parents' organization started in Spain in the years 1958 to 1960. By the fall of 1967 there were 63 local units.

*   *   *

About two-thirds of the way through my tour of Europe, when I had talked with a good many people but still had most of the Scandinavian territory to cover, I wrote myself some questions concerning European attitudes on parent organization and activity:

1. Is it significant that many U.S. visitors to European services for the mentally retarded ask about the role of parent associations? And that while the European officials give polite answers and indicate a respect for the parent

organizations, they do not suggest a major or important role (except, to some extent, in publicity)?

2. Does this tell us something about the relative significance of voluntarism in pluralistic American society, as compared with the state-centered programs of the European countries I have visited? (But compare Ireland: the programs are church-centered, yet the parents are not active in the U.S. pattern.) Or does it say something about European perceptions of the relationship between the citizen and the state?

Chapter Five

IS RETARDATION COMIC?

$\mathbf{M}$RS. JOHN HOLROYD is an intelligent and resourceful person. She is a leader of the local organization of parents of retarded children in Oxford, England, and when I wrote her that I would be visisting England as part of my five-country inquiry into public attitudes toward mental retardation, she offered a series of appropriate suggestions and proceeded to make all the arrangements for me.

The most imaginative of her ideas was that we go together to see "A Day in the Death of Joe Egg." It is a play about mental retardation. The drama revolves around a ten-year-old girl who is severely retarded and spastic. During most of the time she is on stage, she sits limply in a wheelchair or lies inert on a chaise longue. Her "lines" consist of occasional moans and grunts. The dramatic action, of course, occurs principally between the child's mother and father, and secondarily with the grandmother and other adults. The most astonishing thing about the play is that it is a comedy, and a successful one. As Mrs. Holroyd wrote me when she originally suggested the theater party:

> You have told me that your main interest lies in exploring "the status of public attitudes" and it has occurred to me that there may be an opportunity of doing just this in a very concentrated way. There is in London at the moment a play called "A Day in the Death of Joe Egg" which is about a couple with a profoundly retarded spastic child. Incredible as it may seem the author (who himself has such a child) has achieved "putting across" many of the desperate problems inherent in such a situation by the means of laughter—not the explosions of acute embarrassment that might so easily have been

engendered, but the sort of mirth that puts the audience right on the side of the participants and therefore receptive to the message involved. This I think is a fascinating play, and if you could possibly fit it in you would be amply rewarded by talking to other members of the audience in the interval and at the end.

The idea was intriguing, and my wife and I accepted Mrs. Holroyd's offer to make the arrangements and to drive from Oxford to London for the evening.

Without the fact of mental retardation, "A Day in the Death of Joe Egg" would not exist; and yet the interaction of real human beings transcends the particular topic. There are many familiar aspects to the basic theme: self-pity, guilt, remorse and recriminations.

The climax of the play comes when the father reports that he has killed his little girl. Then, after a shocked silence, he confesses that he has hoaxed his wife and friends, that he has indeed not committed murder, and he challenges them: "Tell the truth. You were relieved when you thought I had done it, now weren't you?"

The high tension and intensity of the action are broken by flashbacks and by fantasy. These vignettes are re-creations, by the distressed father and mother, of episodes in the decade of their life of despair, in which they review and lampoon the inadequacies of the physician, the minister and others who tried to be helpful but did not know how.

Startlingly, the severely handicapped little girl dances lightly onto the stage at one point and in the best elocution of a well-trained English child, recites some bright message. Then she disappears into the wings, and it is evident that we have seen only a parent's hopeful fantasy.

In view of the subject of my study, public attitudes on mental retardation, I was impressed to note that the audience seemed at once sober in response to the seriousness of the theme and gay in reaction to the light, deft performance. During the intermission, the members of our party accosted others in the audience and interviewed them briefly, by ones and twos. The results were illuminating. Everyone seemed to accept the play as theater, to judge it as such, and to find it successful.

Among those with whom we talked were two mothers of school-age children, who said they were thankful that their youngsters had no more serious problems than low marks; a woman physician, whose interest was partly clinical but largely intellectual; and a young couple (the man thought it was "pure entertainment," and his companion said it "wasn't at all nasty"). Apparently most of the notices about the play had been favorable, both the reviews and the interviews on television. The physician said she had been attracted by an unusually perceptive criticism in the *Illustrated London News*. Some came because of the reputation of Joe Melia, who played the father, and other members of the cast. One couple turned out to be fellow-Americans, from Toledo. They had read about the play and wanted to see it, but the ticket agent told them it was "in bad taste, and no way to spend an evening." They insisted on going and told us they liked the play very much and were annoyed at the ticket agent because of her unsolicited comment.

*   *   *

After a brief report, somewhat along the foregoing lines, had appeared in *Children Limited*, the newspaper of the National Association for Retarded Children, I received a brief, bitter note from a friend: "The opinion of two Seattle parents who also saw 'A Day in the Death of Joe Egg' was that while the first act was quite amusing; the drama, suggestiveness and spirit of hopelessness, made the second act most depressing. We left the theater with a distinct feeling of depression. Perhaps it was because the child in the play was so much like our own."

For parents who must enact the principal roles for the rest of their own lives, the play certainly cannot seem comic. Yet what impressed me about the production itself and about the audience reactions I observed was that what is essentially a profoundly tragic experience can become an ennobling and enlightening evening in the theater.

Life Magazine devoted three pages to the play and its author, who was the father of a severely handicapped child; the headline was "Making comedy out of a family tragedy." When the play opened on Broadway some months later, the *New York Times* critic, Clive Barnes, also referred to it as a comedy and observed: " 'Joe Egg' is an immensely moving, even profound play about love and marriage. No, it's not funny—it has wit, a bitter, excoriating wit. No, it's not tragic— it is ironic. . . .What 'Joe Egg' attempts, and I think, to a surprising extent achieves, is the analysis of a relationship, the dissection of human feeling, the laying bare of people."

That such a play could have been written and produced, that an audience (unfamiliar with mental retardation as a personal problem) could accept it as an entertainment and that a professional and sensitive reviewer should have focused on the universal aspects of the human relationships are perhaps clues to the status of mental retardation (more in England than in the United States) as a social reality today. From this I take hope.

Chapter Six

INTEGRATION VS. SPECIALIZED
SERVICES

WHEN THE Newsom Commission, in July 1968, recommended that the private boarding schools of England give half their places to students to be sent there at public expense, the proposal was one more expression of a trend toward democratization—may an American observer use the word integration?—of British education.

Almost a year earlier, when I was in England, public interest was churning over the issue of comprehensive schools. At the time, I saw analogies, both symbolic and literal, between the topic then in controversy and the subject of special-educational services for handicapped children. Both dealt with the desirability of separating-vs-merging the exceptional and the "normal."

The purpose of my trip was to study public attitudes on mental retardation. Before I could get fairly into my subject, I found, in the London press and in conversations with educators, an overriding concern with the issue of whether England's traditional separation of the school population above age eleven should give way to heterogeneous grouping in common schools.

Parliament had set the new direction more than a year previous by providing that local education authorities might educate English youngsters in a single school system, rather than in the separate programs which go back some four hundred years. On the face of it, the issue was whether English youngsters should be educated together, from the age eleven onward, or whether the traditional British method of separating school children according to their abilities should continue.

(The "streaming" method in the lower grades did separate the children by academic ability within the schools they attended together. England's "streaming" is similar to the "tracking" system in use in many American high schools, and in the lower grades as well. The concept of "ability groupings," while it has educational validity, does carry implications of discrimination—segregation?—along social lines as well.)

While the separation of English grammar school students from those attending "secondary modern" was ostensibly determined on the basis of academic ability, in reality there was a large component of social discrimination, as the children of the upper-income and better-educated families generally found their way into the academically oriented schools, while the children of working class parents were directed to the vocational schools. Parent resistance to Parliament's action, therefore, although addressed to the merits of the situation, contained an element of what might be called snobbery, or at least a drive toward exclusiveness.

Against this background, when I arrived in England I found the issue of "comprehensive schools" quite hot. Parents in a middle-class area of Greater London had brought a lawsuit to prevent the merger of two schools. During my short visit, the High Court rendered a decision on one of the cases, holding that the British Secretary for Education and Science had not allowed enough time for objections to the specific proposal, and making him liable for the court costs.

The decision was intensely significant in at least one respect beyond the immediate issue: It was apparently the first time in the long history of British jurisprudence that a court had chosen to interpret a legislative act. This is of course a commonplace in the American system of checks and balances, but for England it was a revolutionary development. The London *Sunday Telegraph* commented: "When the Executive uses its immense resources in an attempt to frustrate the Judiciary, the consensus on which our tolerant society should rest is threatened. There is no good reason why, on the question of comprehensive education, any such confrontation should have occurred. Parliament has the last word on this and all other matters, and so, in consequence, have the Government of the day."[1]

The excitement over the issue of comprehensive schools has extra interest for those of us concerned with special education, because there was concurrently a continuing controversy in England over the appropriate jurisdiction for education of the mentally retarded—and the allied issue of whether retarded children ought to be educated in the common schools at all.

Under British law and administrative practice, at the time of my visit, the children called Educationally Subnormal (ESN) were the responsibility of the school and, nationally, of the Department of Education and Science; the children labeled Severely Subnormal (SSN) were under the jurisdiction of the health authorities, even for their training. Many educators and parents believed the children would learn more and grow to higher levels of capability if they were all served under the auspices of the Department of Education.[2] This issue, of course, has its counterparts in various of the United States, and especially in relation to educational programs in state institutions.

There are other curious and ironic parallels, and also contrasts. To the extent that mentally retarded children have been educationally integrated in the public schools of the United States, it has been in substantial degree as a result

---

[1] "School Scandal," *Sunday Telegraph,* September 17, 1967, p. 14.

[2] In November 1968, more than a year after my visit, the Prime Minister announced to Parliament that the responsibility for education of the Severely Subnormal would be transferred from Health to the education authorities. Teacher training and other "tooling up" efforts began, and the changeover became effective April 1, 1971.

of parental pressures.[3] Sporadically, and with greater or less intensity in various situations around the country, there has been some resistance on the part of parents of "normal" children. The same seems to obtain in England. Now, I found, parents of "superior" children (who, after all, are likewise "exceptional") were opposing integration.

Middle-class English parents, I was told by Mrs. Margaret Crozier of the National Society for Mentally Handicapped Children (NSMHC), resist placement of their youngsters in the ESN classes. One reason is that many parents do not accept the evaluation that their child is as handicapped as others believe. More important, however, is the fact that social deprivation is a significant factor in the ESN group, and the middle-class parents are reluctant for their children to be with those of other social levels. Their feelings are articulated in such expressions as "rougher children" and "we don't like their accents." To some extent, though, "mental handicap tends to erase our class prejudices," Mrs. Crozier said.

The controversy over whether Education of Health should have jurisdiction over training of the SSN children extended even to the closest friends of the retarded. The professionals favored the educational setting and auspices; the NSMHC was divided.

What intrigued me as I observed the controversy over

---

[3] An American educator reviewing this section questioned the assertion. Tributes to the impact of parent and citizen organizations appear in "Mental Retardation" in *Social Work Year Book 1960,* pp. 395–403; DiMichael, Salvatore G.: "Implications of Mental Retardation," in Rothstein, Jerome H.: *Mental Retardation,* pp. 101–106; Williams, Harold M., and Wallin, J. E. Wallace: "Education of the Severely Retarded Child," in Rothstein, *op. cit.,* pp. 336 f.; the introduction to "Parent Counseling," in Rothstein, *idem,* 451; President's Panel on Mental Retardation: *A Proposed Program for National Action to Combat Mental Retardation,* pp. 101–111, p. 17; "Community Organization for the Mentally Retarded," *Community Organization, 1959,* pp. 108–121; Katz, Alfred H.: *Parents of the Handicapped,* pp. 82, 132; Segal, Robert M.: *Mental Retardation and Social Action: A Study of the Associations for Retarded Children as a Force for Social Change,* 1970.

"comprehensive schools" and the High Court's decision in the Enfield case was the obvious analogy to the position of special-education services for the mentally subnormal. The question, in relation to the subject of my study, was what implications does this have for placement of special classes for retarded children in the regular schools? And might it affect the efforts of some educators and parents to bring the SSN activity centers (along with the ESN program) under the Department of Education and Science?

David Bilovsky, professor of psychology at the University of Southern California, spent a year in England and studied the educational and sociological patterns much more closely than I was able to do. Reacting to my observations, he commented that English education in the nineteenth century was concerned only with the development of two groups: a large segment of the population with minimal literacy, ready to accept their place in the industrial workshops at a very early age, and a small group, moving in the direction of classical education. In this frame of reference, he noted, there are many who feel that special education does not belong in the schools at all. Moreover, he observed that England has had a strong hospital or institutional program for the retarded; and the status of the Medical Officer of Health, in each county, is such that responsibility for the retarded has been seen as basically a medical concern.

M. Stephen Lilly, research coordinator of the Northwest Regional Special Education Instructional Materials Center, has asserted that "traditional special education services as represented by self-contained special classes should be discontinued for all but the severely impaired." [4] He adduces statements from more than a half-dozen eminent figures in special education over the past decade, indicating that the field is not special, nor, often, does it educate. [5] Professor

---

[4] Lilly, M. Stephen: "Special Education: A Teapot in a Tempest," *Exceptional Children*, September 1970, p. 43.

[5] *Ibid.*, pp. 44–45.

Lilly subsequently elaborated his position in a talk to the leading professional organization in the field:

> Special education can no longer be a permanent source of complete educational services for children. We must become a support service for the regular classroom teacher, dealing with specific problem situations at given points in time, rather than serving as a repository for children from whom a teacher feels she needs relief.
>
> A second requirement of the new special education system is that it must be a "zero-reject" system. By this I mean that once a child is admitted into a regular class program within a school, it must be impossible to administratively separate him from that program for any reason.[6]

The issues which attracted attention in England in September 1967—segregation, separation, tracking, academic qualifications, and social distinctions—received new emphasis in the United States in the school year 1968-69 and subsequently. Colleges and high schools alike were rent by controversy and confrontation, and the issues on the campuses resembled the ones which troubled England during the visit a year earlier—for example, the demands of the Black Student Union for larger ethnic representation in the student bodies, on the faculties, and on the governing boards, the agreement reached (and rejected) at the City College of New York for a dual admission system to accommodate inadequately prepared graduates of some city high schools, the student sit-in (and the parental concern) over discriminatory "tracking" in the suburban school system my own children attended.

The thrust is toward reorganization of the public school structure in the United States to the end that equal educaional opportunity shall become a working reality. Whatever the excesses of protestant behavior in reaching that end, the goal itself is desirable. Once achieved, it will give new hope also to the children who need special education.

---

[6] Lilly, M. Stephen: "Synergy for What?" paper presented at Northwest Regional Conference, Council for Exceptional Children, October 1970, p. 3. (Mimeographed.)

Chapter Seven

ATTITUDES OF THE MEDIA

WITHOUT PUSHING the point too far, it is safe to say that one revealing window on the subject of public attitudes is the press.

Scanning the European press, radio and television offered useful clues, not only in the specific content, but also the frequency of mention, the prominence given to the subject of mental retardation and the use of pictures. The best sources of information were the journalists themselves, and secondarily the people working in mental retardation who conveyed their own impressions.

France was not one of the countries where I made a direct study of national attitudes on mental retardation, and the several days spent at the International Congress at Montpellier certainly did not provide a fair sampling of the French press. Nevertheless, the Congress itself provided an opportunity to get a revealing glimpse of how the non-metropolitan newspaper confronts mental retardation.

Here was an international conference, in a small university town in southern France. Some 1,600 delegates and guests, including world-famous professors, research workers and public officials, participated in the twelve-day conference. The daily newspaper *Midi Libre*, which serves the Mediterranean region, devoted a great deal of space to the Congress. On the opening day, there were articles and pictures filling more than a page of the paper.

The quality of coverage, however, was reminiscent of the small-town American newspapers of the early 1950's. While the amount of space was extensive, and the tone of the articles was sympathetic and supportive, the level of the material was quite elementary. There was great respect for the dignitaries whose names were associated with the conference: the patronage of President de Gaulle, a message from Pope Paul VI, a photograph of Mrs. Hubert H. Humphrey, reports of program sessions involving "les plus hautes personnalités du monde scientifique international." As to the subject matter itself, however, the factual information *Midi Libre* offered its readers consisted of wide-eyed restatement of simple material on the causes and incidence of mental retardation and the moral desirability of helping the retarded.

Everywhere, on the part of public officials and leaders of citizen organizations, I found a recognition of the importance of public opinion and the significant role of the mass and specialized media. The effective utilization of the media's strengths, however, varied from country to country, as well as from individual to individual.

In Ireland, the attitude toward public interpretation of mental retardation was at the level which characterized the movement in the United States when the National Association for Retarded Children was just getting started. That is, there was a recognition of the importance of public understanding, and a commitment on the part of the citizen organization to stimulate public awareness; but the sophistication of the efforts and the attitudes of the media were at such a primitive level that a simple mention of the subject in print was an occasion for rejoicing.

The honorary secretary of the National Association for the Mentally Handicapped, Lieut. Col. Joseph Adams, showed me a variety of publications distributed by his organization and placed considerable emphasis on communications. He also told me of an international conference held in Dublin the year before, with eight hundred participants. The sponsors called on professional public relations people for help, and major firms (such as the national air line, Aer Lingus) made their trained personnel available. The professionals prepared press releases, arranged news interviews and television programs, and guided the publicity effort. "The mass media could not have been more helpful," Col. Adams told me. "They see the problem of mental handicap written in to their agony columns. Naturally, the sort of thing that we're doing appeals to them." Working for the mentally handicapped was now much easier, Col. Adams told me, because the substantial volume of conference publicity promoted public awareness and made the general public much more sympathetic.

There is in Kilkenny, a town of 10,000 population some two hours drive from Dublin, a local Association of Parents and Friends of Mentally Handicapped Children. At the time of my visit, it had been in existence only a few months. A high priority of the organization, expressed repeatedly by the chairman and members of the group with whom I met, was public understanding and acceptance. "In this country," the chairman commented, "we don't talk enough about mental retardation; it's not put in front of us enough; it doesn't appear frequently enough in our newspapers and on our television."[1] With great pride, he showed me an article about the local school for handicapped children. It had just been published in *Irish Spotlight*, a Dominican publication, and he hoped it might be reprinted for nationwide distribution. As in France, I felt that while the published material was positive in tone and would be of some value in alerting the average

---

[1] It appeared that Ireland generally was newly sensitive to the uses and methods of publicity as they have been developed in the United States during the past several decades. While I was in Dublin, the current issue of *Business and Finance*, "Ireland's only financial weekly," devoted its cover and a long article to "Ireland's Image Builders"—the public relations people. Another article in the same issue dealt with a related problem, attracting tourists to Ireland. And in an interview in the *Irish Independent*, a Dublin newspaper, the same week, an Irish priest recently returned from a seven-month lecture tour of the United States and Canada remarked on the poor impression of Ireland which he found in his American travels and suggested, "This is something our advertising and publicity people should examine and look into." With all this concern over "images," it is not surprising that the parents and friends of the mentally retarded should likewise be alert to the importance of publicity.

citizen to the problem, it barely began to open up the difficult and subtle task of communication, which is one avenue to the modification of attitudes. The publication offered facts on mental retardation, but it did not address itself to the underlying fears and preconceptions which characterized the average citizen, whether in Ireland or America.

An attitude which I found prevalent in most of the countries I visited was pithily expressed in an editorial in the *Birmingham Post* a few years ago: "The immediate need is for money; the enduring need is for understanding, sympathy and encouragement." The statement was quoted approvingly in the January 1965 newsletter of the National Society for Mentally Handicapped Children of England, and it may be assumed this still represents the official as well as the popular consensus.

In England, there has been substantial impact on public awareness over the years because there are two national organizations with considerable experience and sophistication: the National Association for Mental Health, which for years was the only organization in the fields of mental illness and retardation, and the National Society for Mentally Handicapped Children, which is newer but has been quite active in recent years. Both have developed a variety of publications, graphics and other interpretive materials and have worked effectively with the press. The major English newspapers have nationwide circulation, so that the efforts invested in London have an impact throughout the country.

One of the publications given to me when I visited the NSMHC office in London was a four-page reprint from the *Times* Educational Supplement of July 8, 1960. Under the bold heading "Ineducable?" it offered a series of articles and pictures on education of mentally handicapped (the English word for retarded) children. The leadoff article, by Mrs. Margaret Crozier, of the National Society, was entitled "New Attitudes." Mrs. Crozier cautioned me that the reprint, being more than seven years old, was in some respects quite out of date. The tenor of the 1960 publication, however, was that the label "ineducable" was most inappropriate, and the "new attitudes" (in 1960) accepted the concept of community care for the severely subnormal.

The NSMHC has spent considerable funds for advertising and publicity, and long-term observers report that public attitudes toward mental handicap have changed enormously.[2] Responsiveness is most evident among the educated classes, I was told.

In each of the three Scandinavian countries, it was my good fortune to talk at length with a working journalist. They were Erik Olaf Hansen, medical reporter for *Politiken*, published in Copenhagen; Olle Alsén, editorial writer, *Dagens Nyheter*, published in Stockholm; and Ruth Erlandsen, reporter for the Norwegian news agency, Norsk Telegrambyrå (NTB).

The editors of Danish newpapers welcome articles on mental retardation, Mr. Hansen told me, and they print his articles as he writes them. In fact, the papers publish more about mental retardation than the people are interested in reading, he said with a smile. The reason for this aggressive coverage of a specialized subject, he explained, is that the Danish National Service for the Mentally Retarded has stimulated publicity. He told me, for example, of a recent series of articles on sexual rights for the retarded— a subject which is not likely to receive extended attention in the American press at the present stage of our development.

N.E. Bank-Mikkelsen, director of the National Service for the Mentally Retarded, is "very clever" in getting the news-

---

[2] On a second visit to London, in March 1970, I again talked with E. R. Tudor-Davies, statistical information officer of the National Society for Mentally Handicapped Children. During our conversation, he casually reached into a desk drawer, took out a small but high-quality tape-recorder, and interviewed me for later broadcast during Mental Handicap Week. I was impressed that an official of a voluntary association had confidence that the British Broadcasting Corporation would use an interview he had taped in his office.

paper to write about mental retardation, Mr. Hansen told me. He offered this observation as a compliment rather than a complaint, and added, "We know Bank-Mikkelsen so well; we cooperate very closely. Actually, this is an important part of his job, and has been since it was established years ago."

Interestingly, a member of Mr. Bank-Mikkelsen's staff, early in her discussion with me, paid tribute to the press of Denmark for its cooperative attitude and consistently positive interpretation of mental retardation. She attributed this in part to the effectiveness of the parents' organization, but she acknowledged that the skill of her chief, the director of the National Service for the Mentally Retarded, was a key factor. This, of course, echoed what Mr. Hansen told me.

As we talked about attitudes of various segments of the Danish population, I asked Mr. Hansen about the extent of knowledge and understanding on the part of practicing physicians. This question led back to the press, because Mr. Hansen observed that so much has been written about mental retardation in the newspapers and the medical journals that most doctors are well informed; and if they do not have all the knowledge required to help in a particular situation, they at least know where to refer the family for specialized assistance.

* * *

The Swedish press is cooperative, Mr. Alsén told me, but mental retardation is still a delicate subject for public consideration. The newspapers print pictures of the mentally retarded, and while the parents do not object, they are sometimes reluctant to have their names printed. Many parents still have guilt problems, Mr. Alsén said, and this at times impedes effective publicity on the subject.[3] His comment was interesting, because, while he is not a special writer on subjects related to retardation, Mr. Alsén told me that he has a retarded son of his own.

---

[3] See pp. 75–76 for my own experiences as a publicity man in an American city in the 1950's.

Mental retardation is not a controversial issue, he said—but it is a new issue to be discussed openly. In this sense, there has been a significant change in public attitudes in recent years. When I asked what had brought about the change, Mr. Alsén commented that a few people had broken the silence; and he made special mention of the books written by Karin Stensland Junker.[4] He also remarked that the average person does not think about mental retardation until he sees a television program or reads an article dealing with the subject. Although Mr. Alsén did not recall seeing much in the press in recent months, this comment suggests that the media do play an important role, at least in alerting the public to the existence of retardation as a social problem.

Each editorial writer has considerable leeway in his choice of topics and his treatment of subjects, he said, although on controversial issues there is discussion with the chief editor.

Despite the informal arrangements, under which the expression of the paper's editorial policy is largely what the individual writer chooses to make it, politicians and people in government consider editorial opinion quite important. *Dagens Nyheter* being the second largest newspaper in Sweden, and a paper with national circulation, the views of individual editorial writers may have considerable impact on the public officials who make policy decisions.

As for his own role, as an editorial writer, Mr. Alsén said he writes about mental retardation only occasionally, just because he is the father of a retarded boy and he is reluctant to abuse his ready access to the pages of his newspaper.

The President of the FUB, the Swedish national association for retarded children, summed it up: "Public opinion is important. The opinion of the man in the street has an influence on the government. We press not only on the authorities; we press on the public too, by trying to get as much

---

[4] Best known in the United States is *The Child in the Glass Ball,* New York, Abingdon Press, 1964.

material as we can into the press, programs on the radio, and so on. The press and radio and TV are cooperative. They do help us. I write articles for the press and they take them. If you can do it well, they like it."

In the months immediately preceding my visit, there had been considerable notice given in Sweden to the special problems of the handicapped in relation to the changeover to right-hand driving. As noted earlier,[5] there had been a massive public-education effort through all media of communication to prepare the people for the overnight switch in driving patterns; and there had been a special campaign concerned with the blind, the deaf, the crippled and the mentally retarded. While this was part of the larger effort on another subject, there undoubtedly was an impact on public awareness of the handicapped as a group in need of special consideration.

*   *   *

Norway was aware of mental retardation during my visit because of a controversy active in the press right at that moment. In fact, the subject became an issue in the election campaign, which was under way while I was in Oslo. The topic came to public attention because of a series of articles written by a man named Arne Skouen and published in the Oslo *Dagbladet* over a period of more than a year, the latest just a few days before I arrived. Late in the election campaign, Norway's Social Minister found it necessary to issue a public statement in which he assured a concerned citizenry that Mr. Skouen's charges were being investigated and that if they were found to be true the situation would be rectified.

In his articles—and I was told he also used television and films to make his points—Mr. Skouen had been extremely critical both of the public authorities and of private organizations for not doing enough for the retarded. Making free

---

[5] See Chapter Two, "Concern for the Handicapped: An Insight from Sweden."

use of such shock-words as "concentration camp" and "snake pit," he cited cases of physical mistreatment of the mentally retarded in special schools, institutions and private nursing homes, and brought charges of incompetence, inadequate supervision, favoritism and homosexuality. He leveled criticism at the private operators of facilities for the retarded, at public officials for allowing abuses and inadequacies, at the citizen organizations for condoning substandard conditions and at the press for not exposing the situation. The main thrust of his arguments seemed to be that retarded children were segregated from other youngsters in the provision of educational services and also that the government should take a larger and more direct part in the provision of services, rather than utilizing private operators and accepting philanthropic support from voluntary organizations.

Such charges might well be brought in the United States— though it is not likely that a private individual would be allowed access to so many columns of newspaper space in a major daily—but what astonished me was the severity of the attack, in the context of a much greater governmental involvement than we are accustomed to in the United States. I talked with a number of individuals about the Norwegian programs and the pattern of services, and I spent several hours at the Ragna Ringdals Daghjem, a private facility for the mentally retarded in Oslo, financed largely with public funds. Brief and superficial as my direct observations were, I certainly saw no evidence of abuse or neglect, and in fact the programs were in some ways better than most of those I have seen in the United States.

My introduction to Mr. Skouen's activities and his ideas came in an interview with Miss Ruth Erlandsen. I had asked to meet a working journalist, to get an objective assessment of the state of public attitudes in Norway, and I had been introduced to Miss Erlandsen, a reporter for the Norsk Telegrambyrå (NTB), the Norwegian news agency. Mr. Skouen's activities were so current at the time of my visit and were apparently having such impact that Miss Erlandsen kept coming back to the subject that was uppermost in her mind.[6]

As Miss Erlandsen explained the situation, Mr. Skouen was writing in a "left-wing" newspaper, and his charges were "somewhat unjust." She said his examples of abuse were drawn from the past, though in the articles I read the cases seemed to be quite recent. The fact is that Miss Erlandsen was not only a writer for the Norwegian news agency, but also editor of *Hjerte Bladet*, a bimonthly magazine on mental retardation. Despite her personal involvement and consequent tendency to defend the existing system, she did acknowledge that some good had come of Mr. Skouen's newspaper writings, television programs and films. "The political parties are now aware of the problem," she told me, "and the national government will be forced to give more money to the institutions." I was impressed that laymen with whom I talked in Oslo were aware of Skouen and his writings, and months after I returned home I received clippings indicating he was still having an impact.

Speaking as a friend of the mentally retarded, Miss Erlandsen commented that "the newspapers are wonderful. If I give them material through the news agency, they use it." Radio and television stations are also interested in mental retardation, she said, but mainly in the sensational angles. (I was sufficiently aware of the competition and rivalry between news media, from my friendships with American newspaper men, to take this comment with a grain of salt.)

After she had answered all my questions in most helpful fashion, Miss Erlandsen unexpectedly reversed our roles. As a working reporter, she asked if she might interview me about my study project, my observations in Europe and the developments in California. Her article went out through the news service (NTB) and appeared in at least thirty daily pa-

---

[6] I did not read Mr. Skouen's articles until I returned to California and had them translated, so that my first understanding of his point of view came through the medium of a critical interpreter.

pers throughout Norway. Then she rewrote it somewhat and used it in *Hjerte Bladet*, the retardation magazine she edits. In both the news story and the magazine article, she placed considerable emphasis on Mr. Skouen's articles and used my casual comments about my observations in Oslo to rebut his charges. Back in Sacramento, reading what found its way into print, I could only hope that the statements attributed to me had some beneficial effect for the mentally retarded of Norway.

All in all, I found the Scandinavian press a thoughtful medium and the writers literate and knowledgeable in their special fields. It was also interesting to note that the citizen organizations concerned with mental retardation cultivate their friends in the mass media and make effective use of their contacts.

Radio and television are national in their impact. Actually, this is largely true in all five of the countries I visited, but it was especially noted in Sweden. With so few broadcast channels, there is little choice for the listeners and viewers, so that if a program on mental retardation does go on the air, it is likely to reach a large proportion of the nation's audience.

Despite the existence of some nationalistic feelings, to an American the Northern countries of Europe seem like a relatively homogeneous cluster—almost as our New England, Southern or Midwestern states seem to an outsider. That is to say, although there are obvious and important differences among the three Scandinavian countries and their peoples, the similarities appear quite strong to an American visitor. The people of these countries travel a good deal, and most of them, including school-age children, are multilingual. These attributes are significant and are mentioned in this context because they have implications for communications. The impact of a spoken, printed, broadcast or televised message is likely to go beyond the national borders of the small countries.

Chapter Eight

ATTITUDES TOWARD THE PRESS: A CONTRAST

THERE CAME to California, early in November 1967 (only a few weeks after I had visited the Scandinavian countries), the director of Denmark's National Service for the Mentally Retarded. A man of international repute in the field of mental retardation, N. E. Bank-Mikkelsen was on his way home from a professional trip around the world, which included consultations in several countries and a five-week stint in Australia. He had only two days in California, but he did want to see typical services of the America about which he had heard so much. Accordingly, it was arranged for him to visit one of the state hospitals for the mentally retarded—an institution which was in truth not much different from others in California or elsewhere in the United States.

Mr. Bank-Mikkelsen spent some four or five hours there looking at the best the officials had to show, as well as the worst. He came away sickened at the "treatment" afforded by the richest state in the richest country in the world to its handicapped citizens.

As Mr. Bank-Mikkelsen was collecting his thoughts for the following day's meeting with a newspaper reporter, he agonized over what he should say. "I cannot tell what I think of today's visit," he said. "It is not right for me, as a visitor, to come to another country for so short a time and to offer public criticism." He was urged to tell the truth and give his opinions honestly, and this is what he finally did. His reluctance was based on his sense of international protocol. In his own country, he would have called in the press without hesitation, even if it meant criticism of himself or his subordinates for providing inadequate services to the mentally retarded. In Denmark, the press is one vehicle for stimulating social action through political means.

When the article appeared in print, the fur flew immediately all over the state, and especially in the capital city. The first reaction of high government officials was suspicion of the opposition party. The governor charged that the tour had been "rigged," though it was obvious that Mr. Bank-Mikkelsen had seen what any visitor might have seen over the past many years. There was an immediate atmosphere of defensiveness, even though the strongest critics of California's state hospitals made it clear that the evils were of long standing and not the fault of the party in power at the moment. Then there developed the rationalizations: "The retarded don't know any better," "They don't really care how they are treated," "We are doing the best we can with the limited funds at our disposal," "Not everyone can ride in Cadillacs," "Some of the retarded, after all, have only the intelligence of household pets."

The comparison with animals was interesting. Mr. Bank-Mikkelsen had mentioned animals too, in his interview with the reporter. "In our country," he said, "we would not be allowed to treat cattle like that." Then he paused thoughtfully and added, "Perhaps you cannot treat cattle this way in your country either—cattle, after all, are useful, while the retarded are not."

Chapter Nine

WHAT CAN WE LEARN
FROM EUROPE?

W HAT WAS THE significance of what I saw and heard during my visits with European leaders of programs for the mentally retarded? Were services really any better than in the United States? If so, was there any relationship between the programs and the attitudes? After my return home, I reviewed the hypotheses on which I based my study, and I formulated three conclusions:

Conclusion No. 1: There *is* a different pattern of attitudes on mental retardation in several countries in Europe; and the difference *does* relate to the higher quality of services available for the mentally retarded.

Conclusion No. 2: The correlation is not nearly as direct or obvious as I anticipated.

Conclusion No. 3: It is possible to learn from Europe and to modify attitudes in the United States in order to improve programs.

There are differences between European and U.S. attitudes, but the differences go to basic philosophies rather than the mere specifics of attitudes on mental retardation as such. The strength and sophistication of parent organization make a difference, as I observed in comparing Ireland with the Scandinavian countries, for example, but at best the associations for mentally handicapped children have a relatively minor role. In certain countries, to be sure, they have a substantial impact on the *pace* of progress, but the *direction* of change reflects other forces. All the national and local associations I observed saw public relations (defined with greater or less sophistication) as their major function;

yet nowhere (with the possible exception of Sweden) are they as effective in this area of activity as the NARC and its member units in the United States. Still, the programs are better in the Scandinavian countries—and in some respects in England. Why?

What it comes down to, I discovered, are fundamental differences among the European countries, and even more between Europe and the United States. Richard Sterner, President of the Riksförbundet för Utvecklingsstörda Barn, Sweden, pointed to some of the important distinguishing features: Sweden has enjoyed peace since the days of Napoleon; as a result of peace, it has achieved prosperity; it has been a welfare state since the 1930's. Moreover, he said, comparing the United States and Sweden, "You do things perfectly (such as research), but your programs are not always as good as ours. This is undoubtedly because your problems are larger . . . You have so many other problems."

He amplified the idea: "You have the problem of race, for instance; and you have the problem of Viet Nam; and you have international responsibilities; and you have the problem of the cities."

All true . . . all relevant. Yet as Dr. Sterner and I talked, strolling across the campus at the University of Montpellier, I thought of the comments of Yizchak Genigar, principal of a school in Haifa, whom I had interviewed just a few hours earlier. "How can Israel, a new nation, with so many overwhelming problems, find the time, energy and resources to concern itself with the mentally retarded?" I asked.

Mr. Genigar laughed. "Problems? What problems? Israel has nothing but problems! So mental retardation is one more. But you know it is part of Jewish tradition to be concerned with one's fellow human being. Those who are basically not equal must have more opportunities, and it is our responsibility to provide them."

Dennis Kennedy in Dublin and the Bishop of Ossory in Kilkenny had expressed the philosophy of the devout Catholic in essentially the same terms. Could it be the religious motivation that made the difference? Yet in the Scandinavian countries, where the church is an established part of the state, pastors and laymen alike told me the influence of religion is negligible in the provision of social services (although in the United States Lutheran congregations provide some of the most effective services in our communities).

Contradictory as it appears, there is a thread which runs through the social orders of Catholic Ireland, Judaic Israel, welfare-state Scandinavia, socialized-medicine England—a thread which is hidden rather than thematic in the tapestry of America. The thread has three strands:

1. Respect for the dignity and potential of each individual.

2. Genuine conviction (on the part of professionals, at least) that the retarded *can* be helped. Among the Europeans with whom I talked, this is more than a slogan; it is an approach to care.

3. Acceptance of social responsibility. In England and Scandinavian countries, the taxpayers expect that the government will deliver on this obligation.

It is not hopeless for the mentally retarded in the United States. The thread is there; it is just not as dominant. In California in 1965, the Study Commission on Mental Retardation declared: "Mental retardation is a social problem." And "Where necessary, the State must discharge the obligation of society."[1] And the governor and the legislature accepted these statements, and they acted.

In other states, the same attitudes have been expressed, and similar steps have been taken. In the State of Washington in the late 1950's, for example, there had developed a "taxpayers' revolt," in which spokesmen for conservative voters asked that government spending be held at existing levels and that no new taxes be enacted. The Washington Association for Retarded Children, at a regular board meeting which came at the height of the movement, directly confronted both positions: It urged the state legislature, then in

---

[1] State of California, Study Commission on Mental Retardation, *The Undeveloped Resource: A Plan for the Mentally Retarded of California,* 1965, p. 1.

session, to vote new appropriations for services to the mentally retarded, specifically endorsing a series of departmental budget requests, *and it pledged support of a tax program to pay for the requested new services.* "If adequate funds for the state programs are not appropriated, these programs for the mentally retarded will suffer," E.H. Riviere, president of the association, was quoted on page 1 the next morning. "In advocating these appropriations our board members felt they had a responsibility as citizens to endorse the tax program necessary to make the funds available." [2]

At the same time, there are other threads throughout America: the high valuation placed on work capability; the concept, still widespread, that the family is to blame for a retarded child; the unspoken attitude that mentally inferior people are somehow less than human, and less than worthy of society's concern.

Yet, submerged though it is from time to time and from state to state, the thread of human concern and the sense of social responsibility exists in the United States. In 1967, the Danish visitor's report of what he had seen stimulated an outpouring of distress and anger on the part of many citizens in California; and some of the public officials acknowledged that the services were not as good as they would wish to provide.

The positive attitudes are there, in the American social psyche, but they are latent, and they struggle constantly with conflicting attitudes. As the bitterly ironic song in "The Threepenny Opera" puts it, "We crave to be more kindly than we are."

In summary, programs for the mentally retarded in Europe are better than in the United States—in part because attitudes are different. We in America can learn from Europe. We can modify our attitudes and, so doing, improve our programs of service.

---

[2] "New Taxes Are Asked for Retarded," *Spokane Spokesman-Review,* March 2, 1959.

Part II

HOW IT CAN BE IN THE UNITED STATES

It is easier to talk than to think.

It is easier to accept than to challenge.

It is easier to complain than to act.

Chapter Ten

WHAT IS A HANDICAP?

"EXCEPTIONALITY" is, in part, in the eye of the beholder; that is, it is environmentally determined as well as inherent. Society determines what is normal, and thereby defines the abnormal, or exceptional.

"In the country of the blind the one-eyed man is king."[1] He is king because he is "exceptionally" endowed. The same man, in the world of the binocular, is considered "handicapped."

For a teamster, in 1902, color-blindness was a minor oddity, no more than a conversation piece; for a cabdriver in 1972, it is a handicap; for a photographer, movie cameraman or printer it is a disability, and becomes more so every year. In radio broadcasting, deafness is a major handicap; in punch-press operating, it may be an asset. A vivid imagination may be advantage or disadvantage, depending on whether one is a poet or a high-wire walker.

So "abnormalities" are relative—relative to the "norm" and to each other. And as the *norm* changes, the *exceptional* changes. The person with an intelligence quotient of 80 may function adequately on an old-fashioned farm, the 90 IQ on

---

[1] Despite the familiarity of the adage, H. G. Wells noted that it is not necessarily valid. In his story "The Country of the Blind" (*Significant Contemporary Stories,* edited by Edith Mirrielies. New York, Doubleday, Doran & Company, 1929, pp. 181–210), Wells told of a mountain climber who stumbled into an isolated area where all the inhabitants were blind. Instead of becoming king, as he expected (for he too had heard the saw), the climber found that his perceptions were less acute and he was less adept than the natives.

a modern, mechanized farm, the 100 IQ in the city, the 110 IQ at college.

Recognizing, then, that it is not necessarily as inherent deficiency but rather the deviancy from what *our* society considers normal *here* and *now*, one finds a similarity among various "exceptionalities." Thus (in the United States in 1972), to be mentally retarded or to be black or brown imposes *social* handicaps.[2] By corollary, one finds that some of the same "solutions" apply to either "problem." The same is true of other physical, neurological and social deviations,[3] but this discussion will deal principally with only two: mental retardation and racial minority status.

The handicapped and members of racial minorities have disadvantages in common. For example, in an economic recession, these two groups are among the last to be hired and the first to be fired. Why? One reason is social prejudice, of which both are victims. The other reason has a semblance of validity. It is that employment opportunities are meager for the ill-prepared, whether their inadequacies are in schooling or in vocational training (and whether stemming from innate inferiority or from discriminatory treatment). The poorly trained find jobs only in periods of high employment, that is, when better-qualified workers are not available; and when layoffs are necessary, it is the same marginal workers who go off the payroll first.

Pushing the question to another level, however, one may ask, Why should these two groups (the handicapped and the minorities) be less well prepared for employment? The answer, again, must be "prejudice"—or, more precisely, "preconception." Here the explanations diverge somewhat.

Most black Americans start life at a disadvantage. In

---

[2] Kriegel, Leonard: "Uncle Tom and Tiny Tim: Some Reflections on the Cripple as Negro," *American Scholar*, Summer 1969, pp. 412–430.

[3] The challenging variety of deviant traits is explored in Becker, Howard S. (Ed.): *The Other Side: Perspectives on Deviance*, New York, The Free Press, 1964.

housing, in health care, in educational opportunities, they are underprivileged. Further, they are the object of prejudice, which assumes they are inferior. Add these obstacles together and the black American winds up ill-trained, and hence inferior (thereby "proving" the prejudice and continuing the destructive circle). The black who can overcome these handicaps must indeed be exceptionally gifted.

The physically and more especially the mentally handicapped starts as an object of pity, but this too is prejudicial. He is assumed to be incapable of holding a place in normal society; he therefore receives less training, or none, and he winds up incapable of holding a place in society. In the case of the handicapped, then, as of the black, we find the same deleterious results—the same loss of human potential—a similar waste of economic resources.

I recall newspaper editors, years ago, who would run any number of articles announcing activities in behalf of retarded children but who refused to print pictures of the children because it would cause shame or disgrace to the parents, or because it might subject the paper to a libel suit, or simply because this was not the kind of picture people wanted to see over their breakfast eggs and coffee.

I recall the woman commentator on a local radio station in the West who was happy to give public service announcements for the annual fundraising event but who would not discuss mental retardation on the air because some of her listeners were pregnant and might be unduly frightened or upset. Five years later, the same commentator was interviewing parents of retarded children on her program and was warning her listeners about German measles and urging that every infant be tested for phenylketonuria.

And I recall a news photographer who complained when, as a free-lance publicity man, I arranged pictures of Boy Scout activities which included Negro youngsters. It was hard to shoot a good picture, he said, because some of the boys were so dark. And furthermore, he said, the editor wouldn't use such a picture. In later years, there have been pictures of black people on the front pages of newspapers across the land, including not only those who participate in street violence but also a White House press secretary, the heads of foreign states, and an ambassador of the United States. Thus does prejudice, based on ignorance, dissipate in the face of growing recognition of reality.

The similarity of society's attitudes toward the handicapped and the racial minorities comes to a focus in vocational training and in employment. As the *New York Times* noted editorially when a vocational education bill was moving through Congress in 1963, "The principal gainers will be the Negro and Puerto Rican youths, who have been at a particular disadvantage through the combined impact of racial discrimination and inadequate skills."[4]

Physical disability, mental retardation, cultural deprivation and racial minority status, are, after all, all handicaps—sometimes occurring together or indeed one contributing to the other. Some, it is true, have an organic basis (such as neurological impairment, or deviant skin pigmentation). In each case, however, the status of "disability" is socially imposed, or at least socially reinforced.

If it is true that the results of social discrimination come to sharpest focus as the minority person (handicapped or racially different) confronts the world of work, it is equally true that the roots start in the world of education. It is in the early school years that the retarded, the black and others whom society calls inferior are shunted to channels of lesser opportunity, so that many of them are denied the chance to achieve their own potential.[5]

It is not merely that the handicapped child and the black child are similar by analogy or in the treatment they receive in many parts of the United States. The point is that society produces the inferiority it affects to deplore.

---

[4] *New York Times,* August 10, 1963, p. 16.

[5] Hurley, Rodger L.: *Poverty and Mental Retardation: A Causal Relationship,* New York, Random House, 1969.

Rejection of the deviant child may begin very early and may be severe indeed. A social agency in the State of Washington, seeking adoptive homes for hard-to-place infants, described a baby with an infected kidney, another with a heart defect, and three-month-old Billy, a handsome, alert boy.

> What's Billy's problem? Nothing. But he is "special"—because his ancestry is part Mexican. His appearance and fair skin coloring make this hard to believe, but his heritage seems to change the minds of some prospective parents who otherwise would quickly come to love him as their own.
>
> Billy is a baby boy, here and now. He needs parents, and he doesn't care about their ancestry. Maybe there's a family that could feel the same way about him.[6]

Language, social class, "race" and educational handicap become intermingled in America's polyglot and mobile society. A distinguished professional in special education, Raphael F. Simches of the New York State Department of Education, voices a question which troubles sensitive educators and concerned citizens: "Why do we find in certain communities a disproportionate number of Black and Puerto Rican children of low income groups in classes for mentally retarded children or the emotionally disturbed?"[7] The California State Superintendent of Public Instruction, formerly director of the office of compensatory education, Wilson Riles, suggests an answer:

> Although most of our children come from lower-class families, our schools have been geared to the middle-class child. Our teachers come from middle-class backgrounds and naturally are better able to understand and communicate with the middle-class child. Our curriculum, textbooks and recognized teaching methods are all aimed at the experiences and values of the middle-class child. But the instructional program that is good for the middle-class child is not necessarily good for the

[6] "Special Children Need Special Families," *Washington Children's Homefinder,* September 1961, pp. 2–3.

[7] Simches, Raphael F.: "The Inside Outsiders," *Exceptional Children,* September 1970, p. 12.

child whose background is one of poverty. The child of poverty has not had many of the simple experiences which we assume are common with all youngsters.[8]

A school psychologist in New York City and an assistant professor of education in the Pacific Northwest, among others, have made the point that exceptionality, or deviation, depends more on the expectations of society than on the behavior of the alleged deviant. Rachel M. Lauer, chief school psychologist of the New York City Board of Education, has observed that "normality is a matter of social judgment." In a paper formulating her views, Dr. Lauer elaborated:

> We have tended to assume that abnormality or deviation is primarily a function of qualities inherent in the behavior itself. . . . We . . . tend to forget that our adjectives are derived from contrasts, from comparisons, i.e. that they express not absolute but *relative* states . . . . Thus, we perceive that what school personnel call deviant is very much a function of what they consider normal or what they think "ought to be." Abnormality, then, includes many elements of social judgment.
> Clearly, both psychologist and teacher view the child against a criterion of what they consider "normal." What is labeled abnormal must be a function of that which is considered normal.[9]

Dr. Lauer's proposal: "I would define our major task as that of helping the normal group increase its capacity to include, rather than exclude, to cope with rather than to reject an ever-broadening range of individual differences." In more technical language: "I suggest that as school psychologists we consider shifting figure and ground; i.e., that we

---

[8] Riles, Wilson, in *The Six-Hour Retarded Child,* President's Committee on Mental Retardation, 1970. The booklet is a report on a conference on problems of education of children in the inner city; and the title is explained in the theme statement: "We now have what may be called a 6-hour retarded child—retarded from 9 to 3, five days a week, solely on the basis of an IQ score, without regard to his adaptive behavior, which may be exceptionally adaptive to the situation and community in which he lives."

[9] Lauer, Rachel M.: "Position Paper on the Concepts of Normality and Deviation: Their Implications for Innovations in the Roles of School Psychologists," 1967. (Mimeographed.)

conceptualize our roles as shifting from that of working with deviants to that of working with the group's capacity to cope with its membership."[10]

M. Stephen Lilly, research coordinator at the Northwest Regional Special Education Instructional Materials Center, phrased the problem and formulated an approach to solution in different language: "It can be said that exceptionality is a psychological construct, created to make order out of chaotic classroom situations. The causative agents of such chaos were posited in children, and special education programs ensued. . . . In order to return exceptionality to its rightful status as an explanatory concept . . . it must be removed from the child. Thus, it is suggested that we move from defining 'exceptional children' to defining 'exceptional situations within the school.' "[11]

Although Dr. Lauer and Professor Lilly reasoned and wrote in quite different contexts, both seem to reflect the philosophy expressed by Joseph T. Weingold, father of a retarded child and for the past twenty years executive director of the New York Association for the Help of Retarded Children, when he told the founding convention of the National Association for Retarded Children, "Although there may be some doubt as to how much we can change our children for the world's sake, there is no doubt how much we must change the world for our children's sake."

The difficulties of children of Spanish-speaking families— and the difficulties they create for educators—are familiar. The language barrier and the cultural differences are among the facets of the educational challenge.[12] This is as true of

---

[10] *Ibid.*

[11] Lilly, M. Stephen: "Special Education: A Teapot in Tempest," *Exceptional Children,* September 1970, p. 48.

[12] Holland, William R.: "Language Barrier as an Educational Problem of Spanish-Speaking Children," *Exceptional Children,* September 1960, pp. 42–50.

Mexican-Americans in the Southwest as of Puerto Rican children in the New York City schools. An education research project of the California State Department of Education undertook to retest, in Spanish, Mexican-American school children who had been placed in public school classes for "educable mentally retarded." The testing instrument was the *Escala de inteligencia Wechsler para ninos,* modified to accommodate the idiomatic Spanish and the cultural norms of Mexican-Americans in California. The results showed that many of the pupils had been placed in special classes "solely on the basis of performance on an invalid IQ test," and that the scores of many of them on the Spanish-language retest brought them out of the IQ range customarily labeled retarded.[13] There are those who believe a similar test of Puerto Rican children in Eastern city schools would show similar results and might explain the disproportion of foreign-speaking children in classes for the retarded.[14]

Educators find that the problems of the racially and the intellectually underprivileged have strong similarities. When the National Institute of Mental Health announced an intensive five-year "catch-up" program of basic education for 1,500 Negro children in Prince Edward County, Virginia, the specialist named to develop the program was a man who had previously succeeded in teaching retarded children to read and write.[15]

Economists agree that the answer to employment of marginal workers lies in employment opportunities for all.

---

[13] Chandler, John T., and Plakos, John: *Spanish-Speaking Pupils Classified as Educable Mentally Retarded,* Sacramento, California State Department of Education, 1969.

[14] A black sociologist with bitter insight and a sense of humor designed a multiple-choice "Chitling Test" to dramatize the culture-links of the standard intelligence test. Most middle-class white Americans do poorly on it. Extensive excerpts were published in the *New York Times,* July 2, 1968.

[15] "U.S. Sets Classes for Negro Pupils," *New York Times* Western Edition, June 6, 1963, p. 5.

It is interesting to compare statements by national and state officials on what prove to be two aspects of the same large social problem:

> WASHINGTON, June 27—Secretary of Labor W. Willard Wirtz said today that equal job opportunities for Negroes could be obtained only by achieving "fuller employment" of the national work force.
>
> "Unless we have more jobs, the cost of eliminating discrimination will mean the loss of a job by somebody else," Mr. Wirtz told a House Judiciary subcommittee...
>
> "The problem of minority group unemployment will not be met until the whole unemployment problem is solved," he asserted.[16]

> No matter how much vocational training the retarded person receives, his employment depends on the pattern of job opportunities generally. Thus the prospects for the employment of retarded workers depend on the availability of jobs for all workers.
>
> This warning was offered by James W. Harris, supervisor of group programs for the State Department of Employment Security, in a talk at the annual convention of the Washington Association for Retarded Children.
>
> Mr. Harris commented that if there is a shortage of opportunities, skilled workers will take jobs at lower skill levels, for which the retarded might otherwise qualify.[17]

That Mr. Harris was black was a slight extra irony. He was speaking as a government official familiar with the job market and the patterns of the national economy.

In exactly the same role, Mr. Wirtz told the Congressional committee that Negroes are concentrated in unskilled and semi-skilled jobs and the situation is getting worse because "automation is drying up the unskilled jobs." The disproportionate unemployment rate for Negroes, he said, had three causes: the over-all shortage of jobs, the lack of adequate training and "the harsh, ugly fact of discrimina-

---

[16] "Wirtz Links Gain in Negroes' Hiring to Job Expansion," *New York Times* Western Edition, June 28, 1963, p. 1.

[17] "Jobs for Retarded Depend on Economy," *HOPE for Retarded Children,* Seattle, October 1961, p. 1.

tion."[18] In varying proportions, the same factors affect the job opportunities of that other minority, the mentally retarded.

Thoughtful students of the social scene, including specialists from diverse disciplines, have remarked the similarities of discrimination and denial of opportunity as between the handicapped and those who belong to minority races. Consider these examples, culled from widely disparate sources:

1. An educator, analyzing stereotypes about the retarded, opens his discussion with examples of racial stereotypes.[19]

2. An economist and political scientist, writing "An Invitation to Action on Poverty," links the causes: "The problem of poverty in the United States is the problem of people who for reasons of location, health, environment in youth or *mental deficiency*, or *race* are not able to participate effectively—or at all—in the economic life of the nation." [20]

3. A state mental hygiene official: "It seems likely that for most of the retarded in terms of the majority of services required, the Supreme Court commentary that separate is inherently unequal is an applicable finding." [21]

4. A social worker, commenting on the disadvantaged status of black people: "Just as it has been necessary for society to establish programs to enable the physically handicapped to compete with the non-handicapped, it is now necessary to think in terms of programs to enable the culturally

---

[18] *New York Times, op. cit.,* p. 3.

[19] Guskin, Samuel L.: "Measuring the Strength of the Stereotype of the Mental Defective," *American Journal of Mental Deficiency,* January 1963, p. 569.

[20] Galbraith, John Kenneth, "The Easy Chair," *Harper's,* March 1964, p. 16.

[21] Klebanoff, Lewis B.: "Facilities for the Mentally Retarded: Integrated or Separate but Equal?" *American Journal of Public Health,* February 1954, p. 248.

handicapped (which is the Negro's present state) to compete with the nonhandicapped."[22]

5. A professor of law went back to the Old Testament for his text: "Defend the poor and fartherless: do justice to the afflicted and needy." (Psalms 82:3) Commenting on the Psalmist's linking of "the afflicted and needy," he continued, "The disabled and disadvantaged are not as dissimilar as their external appearances might suggest. They share a host of deprivations: of education, of job opportunities, of social participation, and of basic rights of citizenship. They have a common need for rehabilitation services. . . . And they have a common right to full enjoyment of that fundamental concept of our jurisprudence: Equal Justice under Law: they who have for so long had precious little of either equality of justice."[23]

A historic decision of the Supreme Court on equal education opportunities for Negroes has been quoted to urge similar equality for the retarded:

"In these days, it is doubtful that any child may reasonably be expected to succeed in life if he is denied the opportunity of an education. Such an opportunity, where the state has undertaken to provide it, is a right which must be made available to all on equal terms."

This opinion was written by Chief Justice Earl Warren, speaking the unanimous view of the Supreme Court of the United States, in the monumental decision issued May 17, 1954, on the cases involving school segregation. You will recognize, I am sure, that this statement of equal opportunity applies to the handicapped as it does to the minorities.[24]

Nine years after the Supreme Court decision, Hamilton Holmes, of Atlanta, was one of the first Negroes to graduate

[22] Simmons, Leonard C.: " 'Crow Jim': Implications for Social Work," *Social Work*, July 1963, p. 29.

[23] Allen, Richard C.: "Legal Rights of the Disabled and Disadvantaged," Washington, D.C., U.S. Department of Health, Education, and Welfare, 1969, p. 1. (Mimeographed.)

[24] Letter to the editor, *Children Limited*, June 1955, p. 9.

from the University of Georgia. A reporter for a national magazine traced the story of one youth's education and in the course of his investigation interviewed the student's mother. "When Mrs. Holmes mentions integration, she is almost always talking about the integration of blind and partly sighted into regular classrooms—a poineer project in Atlanta that Mrs. Holmes, as a sixth-grade teacher, has been taking part in for several years."[25]

A national newspaper put the parallel succinctly, in a two-paragraph editorial:

> Much attention is deservedly being given these days to the discrimination that bars Negroes from entering and progressing in many trades and professions. At the same moment in history another group of persons—white and Negro—in American society deserves to get an even, or more than even, break in employment. These are the handicapped and the disabled.
>
> Figures just released show that in the year ended June 30 a total of 110,136 men and women were rehabilitated into productive jobs under a state-Federal program. This is a new record. The fact that disabled persons can do excellent work is nothing new to organizations serving the handicapped. Employers, personnel directors, supervisors, foremen and co-workers should rid themselves of discriminatory practices toward the disabled. Not merely for compassion's sake, but to help their own businesses.[26]

The fact is that the closer one looks at the social incompetence which some call mental retardation the fuzzier become the lines separating it from the functional inadequacy which results from deprivation.

President John F. Kennedy, in his message to the Congress on mental illness and mental retardation, declared: "Cultural and educational deprivation resulting in mental retardation can . . . be prevented."[27] Years later, under another Adminis-

---

[25] Trillin, Calvin: "A Reporter at Large: An Education in Georgia—I," *The New Yorker,* July 13, 1963, p. 44.

[26] "Jobs for the Disabled, Too," *New York Times,* September 24, 1964, p. 38.

[27] Message of the President of the United States, February 5, 1963, p. 10.

tration, the President's Committee on Mental Retardation reemphasized: "Three-fourths of the nation's mentally retarded are to be found in the isolated and impoverished urban and rural slums."[28]

Health specialists, along with educators and social workers, see a close relationship between social deprivation and subnormal functioning. Among the four "broad categories" of the mentally retarded, the Kentucky State Department of Health cites "those persons who, by society's standards, have been culturally or socially deprived."[29] In California, the State Department of Public Health spelled it out more specifically, noting that premature birth, along with a host of other health problems associated with mental retardation, is far higher among Negroes than among whites.[30] The California department observes the following:

> The majority of mentally retarded, with a mild degree of the condition and no known corresponding physical defect, appear to suffer more from a general limitation of life than from physical disease. Treatment of this large group—a salvable human resource—is apparently not dependent on identifying or removing a specific physical factor. It is even more complex: it requires raising the material and cultural aspects of life among those still grossly underprivileged in our society.[31]

A study in Delaware disclosed that "mental retardation, when measured by means of all four criteria, tends to be significantly greater among Negroes than among whites."[32]

[28] President's Committee on Mental Retardation, *MR 68: The Edge of Change,* Washington, D.C., 1968.

[29] "Mental Retardation," *Bulletin of the Kentucky State Department of Health,* May-June 1963, p. 4.

[30] State of California, Department of Public Health, *Public Health Programs for the Mentally Retarded in California,* March 1964, pp. 10–11.

[31] *Ibid.,* p. 6.

[32] Jastak, Joseph F.; MacPhee, Halsey M., and Whiteman, Martin: *Mental Retardation: Its Nature and Incidence,* University of Delaware Press, 1963, p. 136.

The researchers commented, however, that "the finding of significant differences in effective social level between whites and Negroes is only functionally valid. It need not have a uniform and unmodifiable causal background. . . .The rate differentials between whites and Negroes demonstrate how strong the effect of social deprivation may be on retardation measures." [33] In other words, it's not that blacks have lower intelligence, but *because* they are black many of them are deprived of the opportunities which would allow them to use their intelligence fully.

An educator, Lloyd M. Dunn, addressed the White House Conference on Mental Retardation in 1963 on "A Sociological View on the Prevention of Mental Retardation." He offered a three-point approach.

> First, to reduce mental retardation markedly, we would need to provide adequate health services to the estimated 30 percent of mothers and their offspring who are now medically indigent. . . .
>
> Second, to reduce mental retardation markedly, we would need to find ways of helping people with their family planning who do not want children and probably shouldn't have them . . . .
>
> Third, to reduce mental retardation markedly, I believe we would need to do away with slums. . . . [34]

Automation is often cited as a threat to employment opportunities for the handicapped and racial minority workers. The theory is that by reducing the number of low-skill jobs, automation puts a premium on competence and training, and as the mentally retarded lack the one, the underprivileged black and brown people lack the other.[35] At least one spe-

---

[33] *Ibid.,* p. 142.

[34] U.S. Department of Health, Education, and Welfare, *The White House Conference on Mental Retardation: Proceedings,* 1963, pp. 104–105.

[35] President's Panel on Mental Retardation, *A Proposed Program for National Action to Combat Mental Retardation,* 1962, p. 129; also address by Governor Edmund G. Brown to the California Commission on Manpower, Automation and Technology, December 20, 1963. For a different viewpoint, however, see "Automation Role as Villain Scored," *New York Times* Western Edition, September 9, 1963, p. 18.

cialist in opportunities for the handicapped, however, has suggested that automation may help the retarded more than it hurts, particularly if proper steps are taken to adapt rehabilitation programs to the trainee's needs.[36]

As Whitney Young, executive director of the National Urban League, told a convention of the National Association for Retarded Children, "We should not delude ourselves into believing that society will treat its mentally retarded children as equal and deserving human beings as long as it fails to treat others decently simply because they have dark skin or fails to offer them meaningful help at a time when they struggle so painfully to emerge from centuries of oppression." [37]

The reverse is equally true: It is unlikely that society will treat its racial minorities as first-class citizens as long as it does not accord the handicapped their measure of human dignity.

For those of us engaged in special education, rehabilitation, or any of the social and health services, the similarities between the handicapped and the racial minorities point this lesson: When society affords the opportunity to every child to receive education that will enable him to develop to the limits of his capabilities, we will fulfill our responsibilities to the blacks, the Spanish-speaking Americans, the Indians, the retarded, the physically handicapped, the gifted and—if there are any—the "normal" children.

---

[36] Walter S. Neff, research director of the Institute for the Crippled and Disabled, quoted in the President's Committee on Employment of the Handicapped, *Newsletter,* May 1964. "Although automation will bring about a decline in factory jobs," said Dr. Neff, "it will also bring an increase in service-type jobs. Most of them do not lend themselves to mechanization, and most are admirably suited to the retarded." See also Nixon, Russell A.: "Impact of Automation and Technological Change on Employability of the Mentally Retarded," *American Journal of Mental Deficiency,* September 1970, pp. 152–155.

[37] Young, Whitney M., Jr.: "The Retarded Victims of Deprivation," *PCMR Message,* Washington, D.C., President's Committee on Mental Retardation, January 1968.

Chapter Eleven

THE NATURE OF THE PROBLEM

IT IS SO EASY to be glib about changing attitudes. The obvious answers come so quickly to the tongue.

A West Coast radio executive, speaking to the American Association on Mental Deficiency at its 1969 annual convention in San Francisco, recommended that one-minute spot announcements, to be developed by an advertising agency, be used to create understanding of the retarded. What does this tell us about the effectiveness of the three years of work by the Advertising Council for the President's Committee on Mental Retardation? Three successive nationwide efforts, utilizing radio, television, print ads, envelopes stuffers, transit car cards and other media—and a broadcasting executive was not even aware of it! What significance must the advertising campaign have had, then, for the average citizen of the United States? (There is an answer to this rhetorical question. The public service ads did reach a great many people. Thousands of them wrote to the President's Committee, most of them asking for help for their own retarded children. This was worthwhile, as it opened the way to the provision of services for desperate families. But there is no evidence that the attitudes of the citizenry were modified in any significant way.)

An official of the Ford Foundation, addressing an international conference of the Planned Parenthood Federation in Bandung, Indonesia, suggested that the only way to promote an effective birth control program was to bring strong psychological pressure to bear on people tending to have large families. Among the messages which he recommended for constant repetition were "If you have two, that will do." "You don't need another child now." and "Do you love your children? Nobody needs more than three."[1] This is shallow for such a personal and ethically complex subject as family planning; and the cigarette-and-soap-style advertising approach is totally inadequate for major social issues. Slogans and blunderbuss mass-media approaches will not change behavior that is rooted in emotionally tied convictions. And they certainly won't alter attitudes.

At the annual meeting of the National Committee for Mental Health Education in 1970, I spoke on "Public Attitudes and Services for the Mentally Retarded." In the ensuing discussion, I was asked whether the current terminology of retardation might not be as hurtful as the predecessor terms (feeble-minded, defective, idiot-imbecile-moron) were, and whether the term retarded ought not now to be replaced by a new word. In my judgment, as I said at the meeting, the labels are merely symptomatic, rather than significant in themselves. Another member of the panel, a psychiatrist, put it another way: Deviance, rather than being an innate characteristic of the individual, is an attribute defined by society. Labeling per se, he said, is less important than the attitudinal sets which underlie the labels.[2]

A New York State mental hygiene official, addressing the Louisiana Association for Retarded Children in 1968, spoke of a "reversal of attitudes" and a "growing social conscience" in recent years. Retardates, he said, are now being taken into the "mainstream of culture."[3] Another professional in field of mental retardation wrote, "This nation is dedicated to the principle of preventing dependency and helping each

---

[1] "New Ideas Cited on Birth Control," *New York Times,* June 8, 1969.

[2] The second speaker was Donald P. Kenefick, M.D., whom I had not met previously. He is dean of the New York School of Psychiatry and editor of *Mental Hygiene.*

[3] *Baton Rouge Advocate,* April 28, 1968.

person overcome his handicaps."[4] These assertions are encouraging indeed. But there really is no evidence to support such optimistic statements. Rather, the daily press throughout the United States is replete with examples of society's **rejection of the handicapped.** Yes, people buy Easter Seals and give to help the mentally retarded—but in direct, personal relationships there is still revulsion and rejection. Headlines and news reports such as these typify the American attitude today:

> McLean School Opposed...Neighbors Cite Fear of Facility for Retarded.[5]

> Flap Over S.F. Foster Children...Residents from several middle class areas in San Francisco filled the chambers of the Board of Supervisors yesterday to protest against plans that would permit more foster children and retarded children to live in their neighborhoods.[6]

> State School for Retarded Is Opposed...WHITE PLAINS, Jan. 2—Local and county officials are trying to mobilize public opinion against state plans to build a residential school for the mentally retarded here.[7]

> Neighbors Oppose Retarded Children . . . UNION CITY—A Union City woman's plan to raise three mentally retarded children in her own home met with the opposition of many of her neighbors Monday night. The city council participated in an emotional 90-minute debate with opponents and proponents of the proposal and then deferred the matter for two weeks.[8]

Public information efforts are not enough. From the beginning of its existence in 1950, the National Association for Retarded Children has emphasized public awareness and the need for public acceptance. Some of the most important achievements in the organization's history were the early articles in national magazines, the spot announcements on radio and later television, the syndicated feature articles in

---

[4] Katz, Elias: *The Retarded Adult in the Community,* Springfield, Thomas, 1968, pp. 245–6.

[5] *Washington Post,* April 27, 1970.

[6] *San Francisco Chronicle,* January 22, 1969.

[7] *New York Times,* January 3, 1971.

[8] Livermore (California) *Herald and News,* November 5, 1969.

the daily press, the public acknowledgments by prominent persons that they had retarded children. These were substantial accomplishments for a new, inexperienced, unstaffed, under-financed organization which sought to focus on one of the most sensitive, fear-and-guilt-laden subjects in human society. Working at kitchen tables or huddled over office desks and drawing boards in the evening hours, volunteers such as Gene Gramm in New York, Robert Hayman in Philadelphia, and Eric Sandahl in Bridgeport put their creative brains and hearts into telling the story of mental retardation so the people would understand. Letha Patterson in St. Paul, tapping the publicity know-how of dozens of professionals around the United States, produced "Blueprint for a Crusade," which was NARC's how-to-do-it manual for the burgeoning national movement. Yet in more than twenty years, although public awareness has certainly increased and there is spotty evidence of public acceptance (in the sense of toleration, at least), there has not been the meaningful change in attitudes which is necessary for development of appropriate and adequate programs of service.

On the other hand, there are signs that it is possible to bring about a social milieu in which mental retardation and other handicapping conditions are accepted as variations within the human experience. In Connecticut in the late summer of 1970, two young women were found murdered and a young man severely beaten.[9] There was the customary sense of shock on the part of local citizens, accompanied by fear, because this tragedy was one in a series of brutalities in that area within a few months. But there was a second reaction, a sense of foreboding on the part of concerned professionals, because the three young victims had been residents of the New Haven Regional Center for the mentally retarded. Staff of the Regional Center and friends of the

---

[9] "2 Girls Slain in Elm City," *Hartford Times,* August 13, 1970; "Youth Beaten at West Rock," *New Haven Register,* August 13, 1970; "2 Retarded Girls in New Haven Slain and Man Is Beaten Badly," *New York Times,* August 14, 1970.

program were worried lest public opinion require imposition of a more restrictive atmosphere for the "protection" of the retarded adolescents and adults in the program.

As Joseph J. Colombatto, director of the center, later described prevailing attitudes for me, there was—after the first shock and sense of outrage—an acceptance of the reality that living means taking risks. (This is a crucial implication of the principle of "normalization," as developed in the Scandinavian countries.) Some members of the Regional Center staff, it is true, were so shaken by the tragedy which befell people they had known intimately, that they requested transfer to other Connecticut programs for the retarded. But parents of the Center residents did not demand greater "security" measures; state officials imposed no restrictions on the local administrators; and the community expressed no concern beyond what would have been expected in the death of several young neighbors.

What does this Connecticut experience mean? *It suggests that positive continuing efforts, rooted in reality rather than in publicity gimmicks, can over a period of time modify attitudes toward an acceptance of handicapped persons as entitled to the same rights and privileges as other citizens of our society.* The proof, set in a context of violence and death though it was, is a testimonial to the effectiveness of the Connecticut approach to "normalization" for the mentally retarded.

"If you treat them like human beings, they will act like human beings." So spoke Mrs. Diane Leichman, supervisor, mentally retarded and multiply handicapped, Los Angeles Unified School District, at a regional meeting of mental retardation professionals in November 1967. Less than three weeks earlier, a high official of the State of California, speaking of retarded residents of one of the state hospitals, said, "They have an intelligence equivalent to that of a household pet."

Commenting on a crisis in the New York City hospital

system a few years ago, a doctor whose previous experience had been in South Africa and at the Mayo Clinic in Rochester wrote, "At Grote Schuur and at the Mayo Clinic it was an automatic assumption that only the best was good enough for the patients." When he began to work in the city hospital system some time later, he reported, "there was a basic attitude evident. . . . exemplified by comments such as: 'This is only a city hospital; what do you expect?' and 'These are not private patients, you know.'" He focused on the principle:

> What is surprising to me is that in an egalitarian society with an educational philosophy committed to an ideal of excellence available to all there should be such a striking contrast in the attitude to health.
>
> Could it be that in this land of opportunity the fact that an individual must perforce seek help within a "charity" system is somehow an index of failure and that thereby he forfeits his right to the best in health care?[10]

Attitudes need not be hostile to do damage. Richard C. Allen, Professor of Law and a research scientist at George Washington University, offered a perceptive insight in a paper prepared for the 1969 National Citizens Conference on Rehabilitation of the Disabled and Disadvantaged:

> Often the greatest disablement which must be endured by the physically handicapped is not the physical defect itself, nor the unavailability of needed compensatory devices and training, nor even "prejudice"—in the sense that that term is applied to describe hostile or discriminatory treatment of blacks, or welfare recipients, or people with a criminal record. Rather, it is the ignorance and over-solicitude which characterizes the attitude of many Americans toward persons who are blind, or deaf, or orthopedically impaired: a belief that such poor, blighted creatures as these must be protected from the world, instead of helped to become part of it.[11]

---

[10] Robert W. M. Frater, letter to the editor of the *New York Times,* August 30, 1968.

[11] Allen, Richard C.: "Legal Rights of the Disabled and Disadvantaged," Washington, D.C., U.S. Department of Health, Education, and Welfare, 1969, p. 70. (Mimeographed.)

Most people would rather refer a problem elsewhere than deal with it directly. Applied to handicapped and disabled persons in the United States, this means institutionalization, referral to a specialized agency, or other disposition by segregation. A study conducted for the Advertising Council bears this out. People know little enough about the limitations and capabilities of the disabled; but they are quick to recommend care in an institution.[12] They certainly are not responsive to the thought of working side by side with handicapped individuals.[13]

There is undoubtedly an element of the self-fulfilling prophecy in our dealing with the handicapped. Gunnar Dybwad some years ago, in an address to the National Association for Retarded Children, asked the question, "Are we retarding the retarded?" A writer on rehabilitation has offered this formulation: "From the sociological view, a disabled individual is one who, because of his physical or mental handicap, cannot—or is not permitted by community members to—function in his social roles."[14] It is a social, attitudinally determined definition. Does the converse follow: that if the individual with a physical or mental handicap were allowed to function in society he would not be disabled? And if so, who would be the gainer? So who should take the initiative to institute change?

The Leonard Wood Memorial, an organization concerned with leprosy, sponsored a seminar a couple of years ago on "Combating Stigma Resulting from Deformity and Disease." The stated aim, which pointed the arrow at the proper target, was "to find ways to alter public attitudes in order to reduce

---

[12] "Summary Report of a Study on the Problems of Rehabilitation for the Disabled," conducted for Warwick & Legler on behalf of the Advertising Council by Roper Research Associates, Washington, D.C., U.S. Department of Health, Education, and Welfare (undated) pp. 8, 21.

[13] *Ibid.*, p. 23.

[14] Myers, Jerome K.: "The Prophetic Mission of Rehabilitation: Curse or Blessing?" *Journal of Rehabilitation,* January-February 1968, p. 27.

social stigma of certain disabilities, rather than deal with the effect of stigma on the individual." One of the questions considered, a crucial one, was, "Do practitioners . . . understand the nature and cause of stigma?"[15] The discussants agreed that social stigma originates in fear: fear of the deviant and the abnormal, and fear of the implied threat to the stigmatizer's self-image. What they did not agree on was how to deal with stigma. The more sophisticated among them, however, acknowledged that "public education campaigns" through the mass media are rather ineffective in changing attitudes. Indeed, some of the "sympathy" appeals utilized in fund-raising efforts may have the effect of *increasing* stigma and of giving the victims of deformity an increased sense of alienation from their society.

Lewis A. Dexter, itinerant visiting professor and consultant in the social and political sciences, wrote a paper some years ago "On the Politics and Sociology of Stupidity in Our Society."[16] Drawing an analogy to a hypothetical society in which physical grace is admired and "gawkiness" is treated as a trait of inferiority, Dr. Dexter shows how societal attitudes contribute to the inadequacy they contemn. His use of the word "stupidity," instead of retardation, is itself a shocker, reminding us of the value-loads that words carry. Dr. Dexter's point is that we denigrate the stupid . . . and that we make their stupidity a handicap and social problem by the way we structure society and its requirements and expectations.

The Director of the Bureau of Education for the Handicapped in the U.S. Office of Education, James J. Gallagher, put it on the line when he told an audience of special educators in New York early in 1969, "It is hard for the handicapped

---

[15] The other questions: "What is social stigma? What is being done to combat stigma? Is the social and economic cost of stigma and prejudice fully appreciated? Do present public information, public relations and fund raising programs tend to reduce or intensify stigma?"

[16] Published in Becker, Howard S. (Ed.): *The Other Side: Perspectives on Deviance*, New York, Free Press, 1964, pp. 37–49.

to get a hearing; once they do get a hearing, it is hard for the decision makers to walk away. But the money is made available on the basis of emotional reactions." He cited Gallagher's Law: "Money is always available for programs that society values." But he noted that when funds are short, the priority is usually "the greatest good for the greatest number"; and this, he noted, means *nothing for the handicapped*. Such is the current value system in the United States, as seen from the special-education summit in Washington, D.C. It is noteworthy that within a year, Dr. Gallagher had resigned from his prominent position in the Administration.[17]

Attitudes and reality, reality and attitudes; they are intertwined. Parental attitudes are important in obtaining appropriate services for handicapped children. The pattern of community services for the mentally retarded as they have developed since 1950 is a piece of sculpture wrought by the organized parents of the retarded. Yet there is a group of parents of orthopedically handicapped children in Seattle who have asked the public school system to do away with the specialized "sheltered" education and instead to incorporate their children into the regular junior and senior high schools. "If they are to move into the mainstream of society and become well-adjusted citizens," said a spokesman for the mothers, "they must be exposed to normal classrooms. We recognize that our children need some special care, therapy and individual attention. But we don't want them to live a completely sheltered existence and we believe they need the companionship of normal children their own age."[18]

The mentally retarded are not alone as the victims of inhumane and dehumanizing treatment. There are many subclasses of "second-class citizens" in American society. Black people, American Indians, the young, the long-haired, the recent immigrants with strange-sounding names, the

---

[17] See Gallagher, James J.: "Unfinished Educational Tasks (Thoughts on Leaving Government Service)," *Exceptional Children,* Summer 1970, pp. 709–716.

[18] *Seattle Post-Intelligencer,* November 2, 1970.

people who honor a different Sabbath or who refuse to eat meat or who deviate in other ways from the American norm, all know what it is to be outside the circle of acceptance, to be denied equal opportunity. But what of patients in state mental hospitals, prisoners (not yet found guilty) awaiting trial, sick people in city or county hospitals and parents of well children in public health clinics, migrant workers in the fields and along the highways of the agricultural Southwest, welfare recipients whose private lives become a matter for public moralizing? These too are among the millions of Americans who are deemed unentitled to the rights and dignity of human beings.

The Governor of California, after more than a year in office, finally visited a state mental hospital, and when it was reported that the grass on the grounds had been sprayed with green paint for his visit, he commented, "Well, everyone fixes up the place when he knows visitors are coming." When patients tried to talk about their problems with the Governor during his quick tour of one or two wards, he had to hurry on to his next engagement.

The Governor of New Jersey also visited a state mental hospital. He was outraged at what he saw: the dilapidation of the physical plant, the inadequacy of staff, the inappropriate treatment of patients. He ordered the situation changed and averred he would return in thirty days to see that it was done. He did return, and he expressed satisfaction at the improvements he found. Whether conditions were really better for the patients was still a matter of dispute in the weeks and months after the Governor's second visit.

The unsettling question is, Which governor more truly reflects the values of his constituency?

Consider these comments from knowledgeable people whose responsibility it is to execute the will of the people (name and place identifications deleted, to avoid distraction):

1. *A Catholic prison chaplain* said that the city provided no clothing for detainees and that many often had to wear the

same torn, dirty, often bloody clothing for their entire stay in prison. (A *corrections official* commented: "We are not in the haberdashery business.")

2. *Another Catholic chaplain* at a different prison: "They said the doctor refused to give artificial respiration until he could get the prisoner's record, and by that time he had expired. I met with a delegation of the men, who said they wanted to see the warden and that their only demand was for a new doctor and for improved medical treatment." The *State Corrections Commissioner*, in a letter to the chaplain: "In my opinion you have clearly demonstrated by your actions that you are a threat to the safety and security of the institution."

3. *A prison guard* said he felt as victimized as the inmates by crowded, unsanitary conditions and bad food. "When you're a corrections officer, you're serving time while you're doing your job."

4. *A guard taken hostage by prisoners*: "I've seen this coming. I think many people have seen it coming. Most of the time committees are formed, investigations are made and things remain the same."

5. *A governor* described migrant camp conditions in his state as inhuman. *A public defender* in the same state admitted migrants are being deprived of due process of law. He added, "It's not right, it's unjust and we know it, but that's the way the system works down there."

6. *A recent president of the American Medical Association:* "Health care is a privilege, not a right."

7. *The attendance coordinator* at a large city high school reported it was not uncommon for some students to come to school for their free lunch and to see their friends, but to skip all subject classes. His associates said the cumulative effects of five years of school boycotts, teacher strikes, welfare protests, peace moratoriums and other demonstrations have led some students to believe that it is acceptable to put other causes and interests ahead of a day in school. *A counselor* at another high school in the same city: "The

truancy situation will continue as long as the underlying social conditions remain the same."

8. In response to a proposal by a state senator that non-felons accused of misdemeanors be released without bail pending trial, *a city councilman* said: "Victims of crime should not be forgotten just because they do not get together and start riots." *A state supreme court judge*, on the same proposal, said the lack of a record of past felonies was no assurance that a defendant was not a risk for bail purposes. He said the accused would "be even more encouraged with not even a slap on the wrist at the beginning of the proceedings." The state senator's implied reminder of Constitutional rights and the presumption of innocence was not mentioned by the councilman or the judge.

9. *A Protestant prison chaplain*: "Overcrowding makes it a hopeless job. It's like trying to put a Band-Aid on a man who is running past you."

10. *A municipal corrections commissioner*: "You get basic reform and appropriate attention only after riots and disturbances."

11. *A gynecologist and obstetrician* who deliberately violated her state's anti-abortion law as a test: "It's always been the laymen who won the reforms."

To meet adequately and appropriately the needs of mentally retarded and other handicapped persons in our society calls for more than patch bandages, more than sympathy, more than "charity" in the secular sense, more than tolerance and doles and favors and make-work. What it takes is a total revision of our society's value system. Until we see the essential equality of every human being, until we acknowledge *and act on* each one's right to equal opportunity, it's all mere rhetoric.

New York's Mayor John V. Lindsay made the same point with different words. Writing on "Poverty and the Welfare Trap," he advocated that the Federal Government assume full financial costs of a revised welfare system, including not only public assistance but employment. Then he declared:

> Such a Federally financed system would solve much of the problem, but the final, most fundamental change comes less easily. We must admit our failures and start anew. We must create not just a program; we must even dare to hope for an entirely different set of social attitudes, which will extend opportunity to those we now regard as cripples. A new program can help provide income, protect dignity, encourage work, and end the disgrace of dependency. But only a new attitude can offer to both the poor and our cities an alternative to increasing bitterness, to the mutual suspicions that so complicate our tasks ahead.[19]

In a budget proposal which approached two billion dollars for New York City's anti-poverty programs in the fiscal year 1969-70, the head of the Human Resources Administration, Mitchell I. Ginsberg, put it this way:

> We have suggested a number of sweeping changes that we believe are necessary if the poverty and dependency of a substantial number of Americans is to be reduced. These changes include the institution of an automatic, dignified income-maintenance system consisting of Social Security for all aged, disabled and blind persons, and a children's allowance for families; the creation of guaranteed employment and training for all persons willing and able to work; a broad network of public social services; and a much-simplified, residual public assistance system for the temporarily incapacitated and for emergency needs.
>
> Even with these changes, however, the real solution lies in substantial improvement in the basic institutions of our society—health, education, employment and housing—the failures of which have led us to a situation that requires the funds for public assistance that HRA must request for 1969-70.[20]

And then Administrator Ginsberg quoted the *New York Times* editorial from the day Apollo 8 splashed down after man's first look at the dark side of the moon: "The real

[19] Lindsay, John V.: *The City,* New York, W. W. Norton, 1970, p. 163.

[20] "Human Resources Administration 1969–70 Budget Request," New York, January 2, 1969, p. 9. (Mimeographed.)

lesson of Apollo 8 is that this nation can do what it wants to do, if it is willing to pay the price. That lesson must be learned and applied for urgent needs here on earth. . . "

President Nixon's proposal for welfare reform, the Family Assistance Plan, ran into difficulty in Congress in 1970. Two authorities on the subject shared space on one newspaper page late that year, and what they said shed light on more than the single legislative proposal. Alvin L. Schorr, Dean of the New York University Graduate School of Social Work, observed, in discussing the plan, "That Americans of all religions are equally Calvinists is hardly a novel observation." In an adjoining column, as if to prove and to reinforce Dean Schorr's statement, Elliot L. Richardson, the U.S. Secretary of Health, Education and Welfare, wrote, rather petulantly, "It is the greatest irony of all that those who attack the expansion of assistance to the working poor—principally the U.S. Chamber of Commerce and the American Conservative Union—are those who should most favor this effort to reward and sustain the work ethic in our society."[21]

The Secretary (and perhaps the President) have not looked through the proper lenses. A Middle-western businessman, David Carley, President of Inland Steel Development Corp. of Madison, Wisconsin, adressing a banquet of the Madison Area Association for Retarded Children, told legislators and the business community, "We are coming to a time of social cost accounting in this country."[22] The Chairman of the Vocational Rehabilitation Committee of the New York State Association for Retarded Children, Thomas Coughlin, put the principle in different terms, when he deplored the "undue emphasis on the earning power of rehabilitated persons" and said, "The primary objective of vocational rehabilitation should be the development of the individual to his vocational, personal and social potential for competence in society,

---

[21] Schorr, Alvin L., and Richardson, Elliot L.: "Two Views on the Welfare Plan," *New York Times,* December 1, 1970.

[22] "MARC Banquet Hears Carley Cite Lack of Civil Rights for Retarded," *Madison Times,* May 6, 1970.

rather than the total focusing on his ability to work and earn."[23]

The question must be asked, as it was asked by an officer of the National Society for Mentally Handicapped Children in England, "Are the problems real?"[24]

Are the problems of the retarded and the other handicapped real? Are we, in fact, asking the right questions? Do the issues truly revolve around funding and manpower and stigma and status and acceptance? Should we be concerned about integration vs. segregation in the public schools; about institutionalization vs. home care; about employment opportunities for the handicapped in an increasingly automated industrial economy?

Are these the real problems? Or is it a question of whether we believe in the worth of each individual, in his right to achieve his potential, and of our obligation to change the value system and the social order to assure that right?

---

[23] Quoted in Weingold, Joseph T.: "Annual Report of Executive Director, New York State Association for Retarded Children, June 1, 1968—May 31, 1969," p. 29. (Mimeographed.)

[24] Tudor-Davies, E. R.: "Minimum Intelligence Workers," reprinted from *Forward Trends,* the Journal of the Guild of Teachers of Backward Children, Autumn 1967—Spring 1968 (no pagination).

Chapter Twelve

WHAT REMAINS TO BE DONE

To JUDGE BY the amount of material published, it would appear that the subject of "Attitudes on Mental Retardation" has been studied to the point of exhaustion. The automated storage and retrieval system of the National Clearinghouse for Mental Health Information, when queried on "attitudes toward the mentally retarded or toward the handicapped in general," delivered printouts of 220 abstracts, from 131 professional journals and other sources.[1] Yet fewer than a half-dozen dealt with basic philosophical, ethical or cultural value systems. With these rare exceptions, the studies concerned attitudes of parents, attitudes of physicians, attitudes of teachers, attitudes of college and high school students, attitudes of retarded persons themselves, toward such specific issues as whether to institutionalize, and whether to integrate or segregate special-education services.

The need now is for *basic attitudinal research*: an exploration not alone of attitudes on mental retardation (because these are merely symptomatic) but on the whole area of our society's ideas (*and feelings*) about man's relationships with his fellows. The study should be undertaken with all the rigorous controls the social sciences can bring to bear.

Some preliminary steps in this direction have been taken in recent years. One of the earliest, in 1962, was "Mental Retardation in Minnesota: A Study of Public Information and Attitudes." More recently (1967) Eastern Michigan University published "Public Awareness About Mental Retardation: A

---

[1] The abstracts, drawn from publications in 14 countries and five languages, covered the years 1949–1969.

Study and Analysis," by Henry Gottwald. A third, drawing on the techniques of the Minnesota and Michigan studies, was "A Survey of Attitudes Toward Mental Retardation" (1968-69) by the Tri-State Comprehensive Planning and Implementation Project for Mental Retardation, covering selected counties in Ohio, Kentucky and Indiana. The Advertising Council, in cooperation with the President's Committee on Mental Retardation, has also undertaken opinion surveys.[2]

E. R. Tudor-Davies, Statistical Information Officer of the National Society for Mentally Handicapped Children, in En-

---

[2] "National Study of Attitudes Towards Mental Retardation," prepared for the President's Committee on Mental Retardation by Young & Rubicam, 1966; and Garrison, Mortimer Jr.: "Effects of the Recent Emphasis on Mental Retardation: An Opinion Survey," prepared for the President's Committee, 1967. Other opinion surveys over the past decade, in the United States and elsewhere, are cited in Belinkoff, Cornelia: "Community Attitudes Toward Mental Retardation," *American Journal of Mental Deficiency,* September 1960, pp. 221 ff.; Gatherer, A., and Reid, J. J. A.: *Public Attitudes and Mental Health Education,* England, Northamptonshire Mental Health Project 1963; Justice, R. S., and Tjossem, T. D.: "Community Acceptance of the Retarded Child," University of Washington School of Medicine, 1963; Dybwad, Rosemary F.: "Public Acceptance of the Mentally Retarded," presented at the Paris Congress of the International League of Societies for the Mentally Handicapped, 1966; Elinson, Jack; Padilla, Elena, and Perkins, Marvin E.: *Public Image of Mental Health Services,* Mental Health Materials Center, 1967; Willcocks, Arthur: "Changing Opinion—Optimism for the Future," in *Mental Health,* England, National Association for Mental Health, Autumn 1967, pp. 14–16; Allen, Richard C.: "Legal Rights of the Disabled and Disadvantaged," presented at National Citizens Conference on Rehabilitation of the Disabled and Disadvantaged, 1969, p. 19; "Summary Report of a Study on the Problems of Rehabilitation for the Disabled," conducted for Warwick & Legler on behalf of the Advertising Council by Roper Research Associates, Washington, D.C., U.S. Department of Health, Education, and Welfare (undated); Hollinger, Chloe S., and Jones, Reginald L.: "Community Attitudes Toward Slow Learners and Mental Retardates: What's in a Name?" *Mental Retardation,* February 1970, pp. 19–23; Peterson, Dwayne D.: "More than Knowing—Clergymen: Their Attitudes Toward and Knowledge of the Mentally Retarded," *Mental Retardation,* April 1970, pp. 24–26; Mittler, Peter: "Changing Attitudes to the Mentally Subnormal," England, *Journal of Mental Subnormality,* June 1970, pp. 3–8; Latimer, Ruth: "Current Attitudes Toward Mental Retardation," *Mental Retardation,* October 1970, pp. 30–32.

gland, has given extended and serious thought to the problems of mounting a significant research project to study public attitudes on mental retardation. Shortly after I talked with him in London, he wrote suggesting a cooperative project to be undertaken in England and the United States.

The idea was subsequently developed by a British research organization, Political and Economic Planning, as a "Proposal for a Study of Public Attitudes towards People with Certain Disabilities." The study would explore attitudes toward various kinds of disabilities, including epilepsy, deafness, diabetes, arthritis and rheumatism, as well as mental retardation;[3] and the objective would be to provide information that would facilitate the work of existing organizations in the field.

As outlined in the proposal, developed in 1969 but not yet mounted for lack of funds, the research effort would attempt the following:

> To describe attitudes, feelings and knowledge among the general population, with regard to different disabilities, paying special attention to variations between the different disabilities and types of disability with which we are concerned, and to variations among different sections of the population.
>
> To probe in depth the motivations and origins of attitudes and feelings in terms both of specific circumstances and experiences and of general psychology.
>
> To study the policies and practices of employers, hotels and landlords towards different kinds of disabled people; and investigate the rationales and reasons for policies and practices in terms of situation and attitude.
>
> To indicate, in the light of unfavourable attitudes and practices and their circumstances, how these could be countered and reduced, and in the light of favourable attitudes and practices, how these could be built upon and made more general.
>
> To find out from different groups of disabled people, or where more appropriate from those closely connected with them, the nature and extent of the problems they face not only coping with their disabilities but more particularly in coping

---

[3] The proposal was prepared at the request of several British organizations concerned with different handicapping conditions. The findings of such a research effort would be more broadly significant, to be sure.

with the handicap created by public reactions to their disabilities.

PEP's proposal presents in detail the variety of studies which would be developed, including group discussions with the general public, a more intensive survey (based on structured interviews) of a quota sample of the general population, group discussions with disabled individuals, interviews with such influential individuals as employers and landlords, and, finally, what PEP calls "action tests." These would involve simulated applications for employment and various types of services to discover actual performance in response to situations involving handicapped individuals.

A rather different formulation for scientific measurement of attitudes was developed by the Field Research Corporation, a San Francisco-based social research organization. Upon my return from the European study, and while I was still working in California, I explored with Mervin Field and his associates the possibility of a serious, in-depth study of existing attitudes of the general public and selected subgroups, on the basis of which there might be positive action to modify the attitudinal framework within which services and opportunities exist for retarded persons in the United States. The Field organization considered the project feasible and prepared a detailed proposal. This involved scientifically designed surveys not only of general public opinion but also of such important special groups as elected officials, educators, doctors, lawyers, welfare officials and parents of retarded children.

Both Political and Economic Planning in England and the Field Research Corporation in California estimated working time of about a year to develop and execute their projects. Preliminary cost estimates (for rather different research proposals, in two different countries, prepared approximately two years apart) ranged from $25,000 to $50,000.

Nothing has been done on either project because funds were not available; the likelihood seems less today that in 1967 and 1969 when the proposals were developed. But it seems clear even with the impact of inflation, that a sum in the range of $100,000 to $150,000 would give new information and insights which would lay the basis for a totally new approach for meeting the needs of handicapped persons in England and the United States. An investment in such a two-nation cross-cultural study, carefully designed and coordinated, would be a creative contribution of major magnitude.

On the basis of solid, substantial information thus scientifically derived, it would be possible to design an approach to developing a new attitudinal framework for human services and human relations in the United States. Carrying out such an effort would then be the work of a lifetime for a good many people, but the benefits would ultimately reach everyone, not merely the handicapped and their relatives and well-wishers. It would establish an atmosphere of greater freedom and opportunity for every individual in our society.

Even without the scientific research which should underlie action, it is possible to take some steps toward attitudinal change. We have, at least, the ongoing examples of what life can be like for the handicapped, as exemplified by what I observed in the Scandinavian countries.

Everyone who preceded me to Europe—parents of retarded children, Missions of the President's Panel on Mental Retardation, architects, social planners—agreed that programs for the mentally retarded, particularly in the Scandinavian countries, were more humane, more positive and more effective than in the United States. How could this be? How could the small countries of the Old World deliver services that were more effective in rehabilitating individuals than the United States with all its fiscal resources and technical know-how?

The reports of American visitors suggested that the Scandinavian programs evinced more concern for the dignity of the individual, more attractive physical surroundings, a higher ratio of staffing in the residential facilities—in short, a greater respect for the individual.

What I found, as indicated earlier, was that attitudes are

indeed different, but not only as regards mental retardation. The people of Denmark, Sweden and some of the other countries accept the view that society has a responsibility for the blind, the crippled, the aged, children—in fact, for all those who cannot care for themselves. Acceptance of social responsibility for all of society's weaker and more dependent members is a part of the prevalent philosophy in those countries.

To me, this poses a vast and exciting challenge to those of us who want to provide more effective services in the United States. It is our task to offer alternatives to the present pattern of social attitudes, which embrace the work-ethic, the criterion of perfection, and the emphasis upon competition as the route to desired success.

In their place, we should work for acceptance of the ideas of interdependence, cooperation and social responsibility. These are neither new nor revolutionary; they represent some of the threads in the complex fabric of American thought and philosophy, and in fact they underlie some of our finest achievements in the provision of welfare and health services. What is necessary, in the new world of the late twentieth century, is for these concepts to gain ascendence over the countervailing attitudes which have outlived their validity.

What remains, then, is for us to mount a massive effort at communications, through all available media, to modify existing attitudes and build toward what I found in Europe. The traditional use of the mass media and descriptive brochures will not produce the desired change, to be sure. By "all available media" I mean more than the obvious (press, radio, television, posters, envelope stuffers, signboards, speakers bureaus, and so on). I mean also the informal media—word of mouth, respected group leaders, and all the rest. And we must involve the schools and colleges, the churches, the industrial on-the-job training courses, the political parties— all the social institutions which help to mold basic attitudes in America.

The effort at communications must be pitched at two levels: the rational and the emotional. The work of the National Association for Retarded Children since 1950, the impact of personal interest in the White House for a tragically brief period, and the wide use of the materials prepared by the Advertising Council in three successive campaigns all have helped to make the public aware of mental retardation and to establish a more receptive and accepting atmosphere. Public opinion studies indicate, however, that the understanding and the acceptance do not go deep in the American attitudinal structure. If American attitudes are to come to the level of acceptance and support which prevail today in some countries in Europe, we have a great deal of hard, delicate work ahead of us.

But it can be done. And it can make the difference, for our nation and our time, between an atmosphere of conflict and one of cooperation and mutual help.

BIBLIOGRAPHY

ADAMS, MARGARET: Social services for the mentally retarded in Great Britain. *Social Work,* January 1964, pp. 69–78.

ALLEN, RICHARD C.: Legal rights of the disabled and disadvantaged. Washington, D.C., U.S. Department of Health, Education, and Welfare, 1969 (Mimeographed).

ALLEN, RICHARD C.: Legal rights of the institutionalized retardate: equal justice for the unequal. *Mental Retardation,* December 1969, pp. 2–5.

BELINKOFF, CORNELIA: Community attitudes toward mental retardation. *American Journal of Mental Deficiency,* September 1960, pp. 221 ff.

CLARKE, A. D. B.: Constructing assets in the mentally retarded. In *Proceedings of the Fifth Conference on Mental Retardation.* Halifax, N.S., Canadian Association for Retarded Children, 1962, pp. 4–10.

Combating Stigma Resulting from Deformity and Disease. New York, Leonard Wood Memorial for the Eradication of Leprosy, 1969.

CONDELL, JAMES F.: Parental attitudes toward mental retardation. *American Journal of Mental Deficiency,* July 1966, pp. 85–92.

DEXTER, LEWIS ANTHONY: On the politics and sociology of stupidity in our society. In Becker, Howard S. (Ed.): *The Other Side: Perspectives on Deviance.* New York, Free Press, 1964.

DINGMAN, HARVEY F., CLELAND, CHARLES C., AND SWARTZ, JON D.: Institutional "wisdom" as expressed through folklore. *Mental Retardation,* December 1970, pp. 2–8.

DYBWAD, GUNNAR: *Challenges in Mental Retardation.* New York, Columbia University Press, 1964.

DYBWAD, ROSEMARY F.: Public acceptance of the mentally retarded. Presented at the Paris Congress of the International League of Societies for the Mentally Handicapped, 1966.

EDGERTON, ROBERT B.: *The Cloak of Competence.* Berkeley, University of California Press, 1967.

ELINSON, JACK, PADILLA, ELENA, AND PERKINS, MARVIN E.: *Public Image of Mental Health Services.* New York, Mental Health Materials Center, 1967.

FISHLER, KAROL, KOCH, RICHARD, SANDS, RUSSELL, AND BILLS, JACK: Attitudes of medical students toward mental retardation: a preliminary study. *Journal of Medical Education,* January 1968, pp. 64–68.

GARRISON, MORTIMER JR.: Effects of the recent emphasis on mental retardation: an opinion survey. Prepared for the President's Committee on Mental Retardation, 1967.

GARRISON, MORTIMER JR.: The perceived adequacy of programming in mental retardation. *Mental Retardation,* February 1970, pp. 2–6.

GATHERER, A., AND REID, J. J. A.: Public Attitudes and Mental Health Education. England, Northamptonshire Mental Health Project, 1963.

GOFFMAN, IRVING: *Stigma: Notes on the Management of Spoiled Identity.* Englewood Cliffs, New Jersey, Prentice Hall, 1963.

GOLDBERG, I. IGNACY: Mental Retardation: Who Says What to Whom. . . . Presidential Address at Ninetieth Annual Meeting of AAMD, Chicago, May 13, 1966. Published in *American Journal of Mental Deficiency,* July 1966, pp. 4–12.

GOTTWALD, HENRY: Public Awareness About Mental Retardation: A Survey and Analysis. Ypsilanti, Eastern Michigan University, 1967; also published as a research monograph by the Council for Exceptional Children, Arlington, Virginia, 1970.

HERRICK, HELEN: Professional attitudes toward family attitudes. In *Proceedings of the Fourth Conference on Mental Retardation.* Vancouver, B.C., Canadian Association for Retarded Children, 1961, pp. 4–10. Also Mrs. R. G. Anglin: Parents viewpoint on institutions, pp. 11–16.

HOLLINGER, CHLOE S., AND JONES, REGINALD L.: Community attitudes toward slow learners and mental retardates: What's in a name? *Mental Retardation,* February 1970, pp. 19–23.

HURLEY, RODGER: *Poverty and Mental Retardation: A Causal Relationship.* New York, Random House, 1969.

JUSTICE, R. S., AND TJOSSEM, T. D.: *Community Acceptance of the Retarded Child.* Seattle, University of Washington School of Medicine, 1963.

KATZ, ELIAS: *Mental Health of the Mentally Retarded,* Springfield, Thomas (in preparation).

KEYES, DANIEL: *Flowers for Algernon.* New York, Harcourt, Brace & World, 1966.

KUEHN, H. JOHN: English parents organized for effective children's aid. In *HOPE for Retarded Children.* Seattle, Washington Association for Retarded Children, April 1954, p. 4.

LUE, MERALD: Public relations as a sponsor of better attitudes toward the mentally retarded. *American Journal of Mental Deficiency,* November 1958, pp. 495 ff.

Mental Retardation in Minnesota: A Survey of Public Information and Attitudes. Sponsored by the Minnesota Association for Retarded Children and the Minnesota Department of Public Welfare, Minneapolis, 1962.

MITTLER, PETER: Changing attitudes to the mentally subnormal. England, *Journal of Mental Subnormality*, June 1970, pp. 3–8.

National Association for Retarded Children: Blueprint for a Crusade. New York, 1954. (Mimeographed.)

National Study of Attitudes Toward Mental Retardation. Prepared for the President's Committee on Mental Retardation by Young & Rubicam, 1966.

PETERSON, DWAYNE D.: More than knowing—clergymen: their attitudes toward and knowledge of the mentally retarded. *Mental Retardation*, April 1970, pp. 24–26.

President's Committee on Mental Retardation and U. S. Office of Education Bureau of Education for the Handicapped: *The Six-Hour Retarded Child.* Washington, D.C., 1970.

President's Panel Mission to England and Wales. 1962 (unpublished).

President's Panel on Mental Retardation: Report of the Mission to Denmark and Sweden. Washington, D.C., 1962.

RUSALEM, HERBERT: Engineering changes in public attitudes toward a severely disabled group. *Journal of Rehabilitation*, May–June 1967, pp. 26–27.

SEGAL, S. S.: *No Child is Ineducable.* Oxford, Pergamon Press, 1967.

Summary Report of a Study on the Problems of Rehabilitation for the Disabled. Conducted for Warwick & Legler on behalf of the Advertising Council by Roper Research Associates, Washington, D.C., U.S. Department of Health, Education, and Welfare (undated).

A Survey of Attitudes Toward Mental Retardation. Cincinnati, Tri-State Comprehensive Planning and Implementation Project for Mental Retardation, 1968–1969.

TAYLOR, WALLACE W., AND TAYLOR, ISABELLE W.: The ascertainment of the mentally handicapped in England and Wales. *Mental Retardation*, April 1967, pp. 23–27.

THOMAS, DAVID H. H.: Cultural attitudes to mental subnormality. *American Journal of Mental Deficiency*, January 1957, pp. 467–473.

VAN PELT, JOHN D.: Parent Groups for the Mentally Retarded in America. Canberra, Australia, 1968.

WILLCOCKS, ARTHUR: Changing opinion—optimism for the future. *Mental Health*, England, National Association for Mental Health, Autumn 1967, pp. 14–16. Also William Deedes: Mental illness and the public: old fears, old ideas, pp. 12–13.

COUNTRIES, PLACES, PERSONS
(On Tape)

MOST OF THE persons I interviewed during the European phase of my study agreed to the use of my portable tape recorder. They are listed below (with the number of each cassette indicated in parentheses). Arrangements may be made for the loan or purchase of any of these recordings, by writing the author.

Lieut. Col. Joseph Adams, Dublin (1, 2, 3)
Olle Alsén, Stockholm (29B, 30A)
Anders Arnör, Stockholm (30B, 31B)
Audience at "A Day in the Death of Joe Egg," London (17)
N. E. Bank-Mikkelsen, of Denmark, at Montpellier (19a, 20a)
Most Rev. Dr. Peter Birch, Kilkenny (6)
Mrs. Margaret Crozier, London (9, 10)
Miss Ruth Erlandsen, Oslo (33A, 33B)
Allan Everitt, Stockholm (30A, 30B)
Yizchak Genigar, of Israel, with Harold Dent, of San Francisco, at Montpellier (21)
Miss Gilroy, Blackrock (8)
Mrs. Gottlieb, Copenhagen (24A, 24B)
Karl-Erik Granath, Stockholm (31A, 31B)
Pastor Andreas Grasmo, Oslo (32A)
Dr. Karl Grunewald, Stockholm (28B, 29A, 29B)
Erik Olaf Hansen, Copenhagen (28A)
Mrs. John Holroyd, Oxford (11)
IASSMD session on guardianship, Montpellier (18)
Dennis R. Kennedy and his son, Loughlin, Dublin (4, 5)
Kilkenny Association of Parents and Friends, question period (7)
Mrs. Koeller, Gentofte (25A)

Dr. Lenstrop, Gentofte, with Dr. Bernard Tesse, of New York, at Gentofte (25A, 25B)

Mrs. Pauline Morris, London (13, 14)

The Mother Who Copes, England (11)

Bengt Nirje, of Sweden, at Montpellier (17, 19, 20)

Dr. Aksel Olsen, Lyngby (25B, 26A)

Oxford City Officials (15, 16)

Dr. Samsøe-Jensen and Mr. Karlsen, Ebberørgård (27A, 27B)

Mrs. Ragnhild Schibbye, Mrs. Edith Arnason, Dr. Hallvard Vislie, Mrs. Eva Iversen, Oslo (32B)

Lars Skjöld, Stockholm (30B)

Mr. Smørop, Copenhagen (24A)

Richard Sterner, of Sweden, at Montpellier (22, 23)

E. R. Tudor-Davies, London (12)

Lennart Wessman, Stockholm (31A)

Among the others interviewed were Miss Joyce Emerson of the National Association for Mental Health, England (by telephone), Pastor Olav Strömme of Kristiansand (by telephone), John D. Van Pelt of Australia (in Sacramento), members of the Larn family, London, and members of the Ganz family, Oslo.

INDEX